I0554807

CONQUER HARD TIMES

By Matt Jordan

Dedication

I dedicate this book to my relatives, my friends, and all readers. I am fortunate to have too many relatives and friends to name, but I will add my wife, Patricia, and our children, Lisa, Cara, Wendy, Holly, Dodd, and Brad. I also want to include my grandchildren, Avery, Justin, Jordan, and Riley, as well as my wonderful sister Phyllis's children, MaryAnn, James, Robert, and Susan. My dear nephew, David Capley, departed far too young.

Also, in memory of my lost immediate family members, including my sisters Phyllis and Rosemary, as well as my parents Matthew and Maria Jordan, and brother, Salvatore, who died at only one-year-old.

Acknowledgements

My daughter, Cara Macari, wrote the back cover notes.

My daughter, Lisa Carroll, wrote "About the Author."

Our son, Brad Pettyjohn, helped design the two triangles depicted in the "Introduction." He also designed the drawing to show the difficulty of getting the power of our spirit, through the brick wall of Romans 12:2, to our body and mind.

Urban Book Publishers for the design of the book cover. I also wish to thank Liliana Dunkfeld for her excent job editing the book.

About The Author

Matt loves to write. After graduating from The Ohio State University and earning his Honorable Discharge from the U. S. Army, Matt completed a writing class in New York City. Several of his articles were published nationwide, including, "Making Your Budget Work for You," in Real Estate Today magazine.

He began his study on how to control our level of consciousness, reduce stress levels, and increase our inner power to use in all his work. He used this subject to draft his first book, "Unleash Godly Power" which has helped many readers to improve their health, happiness, and success. Setting extraordinary goals, he began his ventures in the worlds of business, investments, music, and writing.

Within ten years after college graduation, Matt rose through several levels of IBM management while working part-time to purchase, renovate and sell real estate. Following his time at IBM, Matt created a successful real estate brokerage company that led the area in both listings and sales. He bought the first real estate national franchise in Hudson Valley, NY, as he continued to buy, renovate, and sell real estate projects.

Matt loves to teach and has taught classes and delivered motivational speeches to hundreds of real estate agents. His business experience contributed to his success as a consultant, empowering struggling business owners to maximize efficiency and profits.

Music has inspired Matt and is an important part of his personal and professional life. He learned to play classical trumpet at nine years old. He later added jazz and other genres. He led a band in high school and formed a band to pay his way through college. He later attained his record producer certification in New York City. Several of Matt's recordings enjoyed worldwide radio play, made Billboard, and received favorable reviews. He has had the honor of performing with many renowned artists, including the late Wells Kelly, the drummer from the band *Orleans*. Matt's trumpet solo on Mercury Rev's hit song "Empire State" received a strong review in Rolling Stone. His smooth jazz album, "Let the Feeling Flow" is still played worldwide.

Matt dedicates his time to writing, music, real estate investments, and teaching classes. He loves to teach and deliver motivational speeches. Matt enjoys living life passionately and relishes the happiness his work and service to the community have enabled him to achieve. He lives with his wife, Patricia, in their Hudson Valley, NY home and part-time in their condominium in Florida. While he loves to travel, his favorite times are spent with his family.

Introduction

We all go through some ridiculously hard times. Life is not easy for anyone, regardless of status, bank account, net worth, or anything else. We all get hit with exceedingly challenging times for us to get through. We just are faced with different problems at various times. When tough times hit us, it can feel like a massive lightning thunderstorm, which is why I chose a storm for the cover artwork.

This book is organized into three parts.

The first part will tackle difficult subjects that push us into tough times, like fear, anxiety, anger, depression, and many others. If we address these triggers, some things avoid doing that cause troubled times.

The second part will address how to conquer the demanding times that do hit us. I cover many of the potential problems we must face, along with solutions to free us.

The third part teaches vigilance regarding avoiding demanding situations and adapting to stressful lifestyles to build armor that protects our state of mind. In many cases, it will require a change in habits and lifestyle. I do acknowledge that we cannot always avoid some tough times. However, you will be surprised how many of them you can avoid.

As I did in my first book, I want to make it perfectly clear that I am not talking down to anyone or being judgmental. None of us is perfect, including me. We all make mistakes, but we should always try to do what is right. I have learned from my mistakes, and one of my goals is to prevent readers from suffering some of the consequences of making wrong decisions.

I will give a little preview of my first book, "Unleash Godly Power," to use the concepts from that book and this book to work the way out of challenging times. While I have read books on stress, level of consciousness, happiness, health, and success, I have never seen one that ties them all together, as it happens in most situations. I believe the idea I produced to show the relationship between these four subjects in two triangles came to me from God.

I occasionally read my first book and think, "Did I write this?" as many of the ideas came to me from my subconscious as I was writing.

Everyone needs to understand these two triangles to control just where you will be in your level of consciousness, health, happiness, and success. There is a symbiotic inverse relationship between the levels of consciousness and our level of inner power. As we rise to one level of consciousness, we release a level of stress, and we rise to one level of inner power.

LEVEL OF CONSCIOUSNESS   **LEVEL OF INNER POWER**

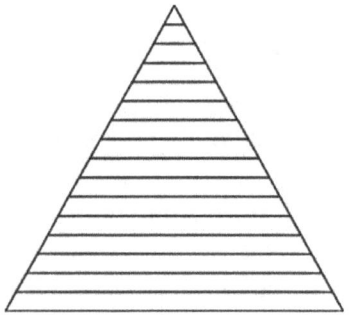
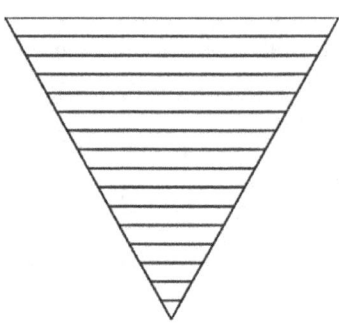

If we take the time to reduce stress levels, we rise in consciousness, improving our health, happiness, and success. However, suppose we continue to develop deeper and deeper levels of stress. In that case, we drop in our level of consciousness, and this negatively will also drop us in health, happiness, and success. This is an uncomplicated way of seeing how our level of consciousness affects our inner power, health, and happiness. While we could only draw some lines reflecting levels, there are hundreds of stress levels. If we are close to the bottom, it can take hours, days, or even longer to move up, even just a little.

At the top of the level of consciousness, the bible tells us we have the same power as Jesus to "move mountains." We could do absolutely anything if we could get there. There we have total happiness, great health, and enormous success. We could feel perfect love, joy, peace, patience, kindness, goodness, faithfulness, gentleness, and self-control, which scripture refers to as the "Fruits of Spirit."

However, at the lowest level, we are powerless, unhappy, sick, and fail at anything we do. We will feel hatred, anger, sadness, hostility, impatience, nastiness, unfaithfulness, and meanness and totally will lack self-control. Many become alcoholics, drug addicts, prostitutes, or killers. Demons take over our minds, and we do things that we normally would never do

As we do things described in my first book, "Unleash Godly Power," we need to work every morning and evening to reduce our stress levels. We can meditate, pray, rest, exercise, stretch, and unwind. We can feel ourselves slowly rising in consciousness and building better health, happiness, and success. Is it that simple? Yes, it is. While the life and toxins we face in the air and in our homes, it is impossible to both get and stay at the top. However, our goal should be to get as close as possible.

God had to place some "Checks and balances" in this, or terrorists could mentally knock a building down. I would advise you to read my first book to better understand all this along with the tools I provide to help you fully control this. There, you will

vii

learn all you have to do to build health, happiness, and success and how to stay high in your level of consciousness.

We all know that we use only a portion of our brains. As we rise in consciousness, we also increasingly use our brain power.

"Life is tough at times for all of us. We just have different problems at various times. We must never give up. If things are getting easy, the reason should not be that we are going downhill by giving up. Persevere in the direction of success."

Matt Jordan

Foreword

Writing a book is a difficult thing, but with so much suffering these challenging days, Matt Jordan's timing of this book could not be more perfect. All challenges must be faced and conquered, and this book will teach you how.

The journey of writing this book has further strengthened Matt's faith in human will. He has come to accept that humans can face up to the difficulties they get stormed with, and if they maintain an honest faith in God and themselves, these difficulties reveal themselves to be remarkably solvable.

The author has found that the greatest enemy of a man living in hard times is often himself – the shadow of fear, doubt, and anxiety that guides a person towards that abyss of melancholy resignation where so many spend their days. All of us on this earth face many hard times in our lives, but how we respond to these challenges defines us as individuals. Suppose we keep allowing these troubles to weigh over us. In that case, they will continue to gain ground in this war – they will continue to overwhelm us, and ultimately, we will not be able to function efficiently within our own lives.

Yet there is another choice. We do not have to live our lives in fear; we do not have to give into hopelessness. Mankind was sent unto this earth with free will – and this will be what encourages us to attain mastery over ourselves and our troubles. Ultimately, free will implies a choice. We can succumb to our troubles…

…Or we can conquer them.

Lilianna Dunkeld, Editor

ix

Table of Contents

Part One

CAUSES OF HARD TIMES

Chapter 1

PERSONAL FEARS

WORRY

Many people seem to wallow in their constant worrying when reacting to the world and the stimulus it evokes. Humans have acute senses when perceiving their environment, and such outward forces mold their character.

One's future is never predictable. A multitude of circumstances can play out, which can become problematic for one's state of being. However, research does not support constant worry, as most things we worry about never happen. We should instead prepare and prevent problems from happening.

"Worry is like walking on a treadmill. You are getting some exercise, but you are not getting anywhere."

Matt Jordan

One of the causes of chronic fatigue is constant worry about events that will never occur. Worrying is a form of destructive, diffident behavior that will negatively impact our mental and physical health, sapping our strength.

2

It will make us restless and jumpy, leading to headaches and stomach aches. We cannot concentrate whether we are still in school or out in a job or business. It will lead to anxiety, which I will cover in the next section.

When we worry, especially lying in bed, causing insomnia, we need to use these tools to snap out of it. We can take some long breaths while we meditate and take command of our thoughts. I like to use a meditation word of my choice and think about it repeatedly. We need to take charge of how we think and stop ourselves from stopping negative and worrisome thinking. I will cover insomnia in more detail later, but "monkey jump thinking" is a major cause of insomnia, and we need to strongly command ourselves to stop it.

"Tomorrow will worry about its own things."

Matthew 6:34

It is a waste of time for us to lie in bed, worrying about the direction we should take tomorrow. Trust in God and let the lord direct your path. We all make mistakes, but we must continue avoiding them as much as possible. We should meditate and pray about each problem about which we are worrying. The answers will come to us but be sure to screen them. Remember, two voices continuously via for our attention, the devil and God. Therefore, always screen the inner voices we hear; if they are sinful, avoid them; if they are righteous, true, and noble, listen to them.

When we often worry about a problem, especially in bed, we imagine the problem to be much worse than it is. When we are going through any problem, it is important to keep the problem in perspective and not 'build mountains out of molehills.'

We will discuss fear soon but let us first examine the difference between worry and fear. We create worry as we decide to fear something within our imagination.

3

Worrying is a choice we do not have to waste time doing.

Part of the reason we worry could be that we have lost confidence in ourselves and in our faith. Once we understand the field of work, we were born to do and get the proper education and experience, we should be confident in ourselves. With faith, the opposite of worry, we can accomplish anything we work hard enough to achieve. We must believe and trust in God to oversee our lives so we will never have to worry. When we have problems, pray over them, and put the problems on the cross.

Prayer can give us a new, more powerful self and help us to avoid being victims of worry.

"If it is a mistake of the head and not the heart, don't worry about it, that's the way we learn."

Earl Warren

FEAR

"I am not afraid of tomorrow, for I have seen yesterday, and I love today."

William Allen White

We fear physical, psychological, and emotional events or situations. Like worry, most of the things we fear never happen. Fear is something that drops on us and gets our attention, whether it is real or imaginary.

While fear is a negative emotion, sometimes fear is important. Subconsciously, it is warning us of danger. The good news is that

4

most of the things we fear never happen. This is a definition some use for fear.

F = False, **E** = Evidence, **A** = appearing, **R** = Real.

In most cases, fear is that way: thinking of false evidence appearing real. At least 90% of all our fears never come to fruition. Those with faith are rarely afraid of anything, and Fear is the opposite of faith.

"He said to his disciples, "Why are you so afraid? Do you still have no faith?"

Mark 4:40

Fear normally accompanies one whose mind is consumed with thoughts of terrible things that we think may happen. If we have a real problem, we should treat it as a challenge. We should research alternative solutions and make it fun to try to avoid the problem before it happens.

To accomplish this, we must remain calm while working out the solutions. However, it is important to do this on a timely basis. Procrastination will only perpetuate what could be an imaginary potential problem into a real one. We must get it over with and get back to living with joy in our hearts. God did not create us to fear.

"Let not thy heart be troubled."

John 14:1

The peace of God is always available to us. We do not have to feel the improper pain handling of problems will cause. We can have peace and feel joy despite the chaos going on in the world around us. This joy comes from God.

5

"The Lord is my light and my salvation; whom shall I fear?"

Psalm 27:1

He wants us to have an abundant and happy life. This does not depend on circumstances or what is happening around us in the world or our family.

We must stop worrying unnecessarily. When we fear something, we must turn to God and trust in His promise.

"For God has not given us a spirit of fear, but of power and of love and a sound mind."

Timothy 1:7

God does not lose track of us. He cares for us. Jesus said not to be afraid when we face tough times. When our fear causes us to doubt whether God has our back, Jesus taught us to have faith because He is in control. He will never fail to lose track of where we are in life, especially during a crisis.

Now, if someone threatens us, the fear that springs forth is legitimate therein, it needs to be addressed, for it targets our well-being.

Does this mean that we resort to violence? No, we must call the police and take steps to defend ourselves should the situation escalate. We should not live with this fear, as many do, because they fear the consequences of calling the police, but you have a huge rise if we do not call-in help.

We will talk about women or men living in bondage and what they should do. Never allow anyone to place you in bondage.

You may ask, "What about soldiers in war? Should they not be afraid?" All people fear for their lives in war. They become heroes because they demonstrate sheer courage as they do not run away.

6

Many fear whether they or their families will have enough to eat. Again, that fear happens due to a lack of faith and trust in God, who has promised to feed us.

"Therefore, I tell you, do not worry about your life, what you will eat or drink; or about your body, what you will wear...Look at the birds; they do not sow or reap ...yet your heavenly Father feeds them."

Matthew 6:25-26

Other forms of prevalent fears thrive on this material Earth, for example, the devil, death, commitment to marriage, divorce, financial problems, and surgery.

They should seek help from their church, a psychologist, or one who specializes in whatever the fear is.

The worst thing is not to do anything when we feel fear. We must not let fear turn into hopelessness within ourselves. This will imprison us unnecessarily and rob us of our joy, peace, and the need to concentrate on our daily lives.

"The Lord delivered me from all my fears."

Psalm 34:4

STRESS KILLS

"In times of great stress or adversity, it's always best to keep busy, to plow your anger and your energy into something positive."

Lee Iaccoca

Stress may take root in our mind, but what facilitates its cancerous growth is how we perceive and process the world. Our perception of the world can either reduce or increase stress levels. It is a mental and physical state triggered by uncomfortable circumstances or stimuli. The consequence of such issues are physical alterations like acne, shortness, nervousness, and to be short-tempered. It can affect our wellbeing both mentally and physically.

People do not realize that stress can overwhelm a person if left unmanaged, creating chronic diseases. We become overwhelmed and unable to cope with everyday situations with our families, jobs, school, and friends. It hits people of all ages, from young children to the elderly. A person's stress level usually has no relationship with the severity of the situation, causing it to overcome us and our inability to cope.

It may cause our heart rate to increase and our blood pressure to drop, reducing our blood supply to our brain. We could faint if we do not take immediate control of our emotions. We should not ignore symptoms like blurred vision, cold sweats, lightheadedness, nausea, fatigue, and yawning. If so, we must immediately lie down with our legs lifted to supply more blood to our brains.

Stress and sugar are the two significant causes of illness and the perpetrator of heart disease and many deaths within our populace. Together, they will cause plaque to build up in our arteries. While doctors treat cholesterol, they fail to treat the core of the problem. However, it is the stress and sugar that causes inflammation to build up in arteries. Then the cholesterol will stick to our arteries.

Cholesterol has an important job in our body in aiding the production of cell membranes, hormone production, and vitamin D.

But be mindful, do not be gluttonous with this gift. Anything taken in excess is harmful to us; therefore, we need to be mindful of our sugar intake therein, as well as cholesterol. We get enough from food, including sugar in the fruit we consume.

It is not advisable to add more sugar with unnecessary candy and desserts, but does that mean you ban yourself from that food item? Not really, but do be mindful of how much you consume sugar.

As mentioned above, adapt, and adopt preventive measures to save you from stress and disease. Your body and life are a gift; take better care of them.

I advise everyone to meditate for at least twenty minutes two times a day to reduce stress levels, raise our level of consciousness and contribute to better health, happiness, and success. I do this in the morning routine, which includes prayer, meditation, breathing exercises, repeating positive affirmations, and reading scripture.

Relaxing music also can help, like a classical piano and other times, people enjoy the sounds of nature like rain, wind, or the crackling of the campfire.

If we allow stress to remain uncontrolled, it will grow and grow. As our stress levels increase, we drop lower and lower in consciousness and in our available inner power. This will lead to a

9

lot of avoidable tough times. It is always better to prevent a problem than to try to solve it. When we feel stress growing inside us, it is time to stop whatever we are doing as soon as possible and go somewhere to be alone to calm down.

"Jesus said to them, come with me by yourselves to a quiet place and get some rest."

Mark 6:31

Keep in mind that stress kills, and doctors do not tell you that as they are trained to treat symptoms in many cases.

THOUGHTS OF SUICIDE

Suicide is a heavy subject. The deliberate absence of one's soul in a household that is now incomplete because somebody decided to end their life. It not only leaves one's book of life unfinished, but it harms others around them because a single life is connected to many others. Like a spider's web, if one string is cut, then its structure is compromised.

Now suicide is the second leading cause of death in teenagers the threat, and we must understand why? We must take each case seriously because you never know when its claws will gouge out the life of someone.

Anyone who thinks of ending their life is at rock bottom in their level of consciousness. Many are trying to decide whether to end their life. To God, there is no choice because He gave us our souls and the life we live. It is a gift we unknowingly squander and disrespect upon taking our lives.

10

"This day, I call the heavens and the earth as witnesses against you that I have set before your life and death, blessings, and curses. Now choose life so that you and your children may live."

Deuteronomy 30:19

When thinking of suicide, we must quickly take charge of all thoughts and immediately change what we think to positive, good thoughts. Remember, how we think will directly control how we feel and how we act.

There are times in many people's lives when they become so mentally undone that they wonder if life is worth living. They even think of committing suicide but remember that there is hope and death is never the answer.

God did not create us to end our own life; He wants us to be happy and fulfilled.

People have several reasons why they get so upset and think of suicide upon isolating themselves from the world and their Lord. We have seen an example of this during the Covid lockdowns, which isolated people from the world and drove them to depression, especially in teens. Parents cannot ignore their children's conduct, especially if they see signs like cutting scars.

"Cutting" is a dangerous reaction and consequence of depression that many of our nation's youths use to release deep emotions through inflicting pain upon themselves.

Sometimes, teens tease or bully each other at brutal levels, damaging their egos and, thus, their souls. It gets so bad for some kids that they take their own lives. I will discuss bullying in another section of the book, but I believe that schools must get very tough on bullying and take disciplinary action. If bullies commit over two suspensions, the principal must expel them from school.

11

Parents must study this problem and react immediately upon catching the signs of bullying. Parents of children who bully others must take action to stop their children from upsetting other students.

This is not just a matter of telling our children to forgive each other, but it is a matter of a child's spirit fracturing to the point that drives them over the edge. All of us have our own demons and an abyss; faith keeps us afloat so that it does not consume us, thus, driving us to take our own lives because living is far too overwhelming on our broken souls.

Children who are thinking of suicide must get therapy from a professional. It may mean the difference between life and death, and parents need to immediately nip the problem in its bud. They should understand that if they kill their body, their spirit will suffer the consequences of their actions for eternity, and as parents, your influence on the matter will be questioned.

Suicide threats should not be taken lightly as the numbers keep rising, and it is a problem that affects us on a global scale. Parents must get their children to help. Parents should advise their children not just to pray and turn to God but to lean on God and know that He loves us.

"No matter what happens or how bad it seems today, life does go on, and it will be better tomorrow."

Maya Angelou

ANGER

"To lose your temper is like pouring gasoline on a fire. Use self-control to manage anger. You cannot solve a problem while screaming."

Matt Jordan

Remember that we can only communicate effectively if we learn to listen to anyone trying to tell us something. It can be a voice or something as subtle as body language. We can often avoid anger if we first know what we may have done to anger the offender. That said, people will anger us, especially if they yell at us before we know what they think we did wrong. When someone offends us, it is natural to feel anger.

Sometimes they cause us to lose money or a job promotion. They did or said something that could damage our reputation. I have warned of the danger of the *"I don't get mad, I get even"* attitude. This is a threat to do something harmful to that person. You are stooping down to the low level of the person who harmed you.

Doing wrong does not make it right. Bless the person who caused the anger. Scripture advises:

"My dear brothers and sisters, take note of this: Everyone should be quick to listen, slow to speak and slow to become angry."

James 1:19

We can communicate much more effectively if we learn to practice silence and listen to anyone who is attempting to communicate with us. Keep in mind that the act of listening is not

13

an easy feat. Most of us want to talk, but very few of us want to listen. When someone says something that is upsetting, we should first consider this scripture.

If we do that, we can usually brush it off by saying that the abuser is not a good person. Read the source that I provided above and re-read the sentence above. One should never jump to conclusions without knowing the full story from all sides. In any case, we must forgive the other person, which is not only the best route of action, but you become the bigger person for doing so.

Why keep grudges and fight for eternity when you can extend a bridge of compromise and friendship for a fulfilling relationship? If we let others and problems offend us, we are wasting a lot of time being angry. We cannot feel happiness, peace, and calm if we are angry.

We should, instead, practice self-control. We need to learn to bounce away all negativities from our minds and from the sources acting out of our control. Ignore them and do not accept nor facilitate their behavior by acting against them akin to pouring fuel on raging flames.

We should build the shield of Godly armor all around us. If we become angry with others, while it is difficult, we should remember what God wants us to do.

"The Lord is slow to anger, abounding in love and forgiving sin and rebellion. Yet He does not leave the guilty unpunished."

Numbers 14:18

It is easier to do this when we remind ourselves that vengeance is God's, and He always takes it to evil people. I admit it is hard to love our enemies or anyone who gets us angry. Admittedly, that is exceedingly difficult for me to do. However, I try to think about that and work on it, which could take days. A good start is to

14

forgive others when someone starts yelling at us. Use this alternative other than to anger. Throw the offender off by shocking them as they expect you to be angry and fight them. Instead, calm them down immediately by doing this. Speak to them very softly. Say something like,

"I am sorry I made you feel that way. I did not mean to do that."

It can quickly turn the other's wrath into butter. I have done it, and it works. It sure is better than getting your blood pressure up by getting into a fight that nobody ever wins, and you may lose a few precious teeth.

"A gentle answer turns away wrath, but an as harsh word stirs up anger."

Proverbs 15:1

When we allow our anger to simmer, day after day, it turns to bitterness which will hold us back from being healthy, happy, and successful. To forgive is a huge part of getting over our anger with others.

"In fact, not forgiving is like drinking rat poison and then waiting for the rat to die."

Anne Lamott

15

Chapter 2

FAULTY THINKING

FEAR OF THE APOCALYPSE

The world is in chaos right now, and many people are worried about the apocalypse predicted in the Bible. This worry causes us to experience unnecessarily tough times because it makes us feel negative and worried. We may even feel depressed and hopeless. This is not what God wants for any of us. The fear of the Apocalypse has scared many of us for many years.

It is a meme, which has become a world phenomenon, passed on through many generations. The first apocalyptic meme, predicting the end of the world, started two thousand years ago in an area now called Iran. It never happened. Many writers from then on started new versions of the same meme creating apocalyptic dates that never happened.

In 1999, Y2K, the year 2000 became another meme that predicted an apocalypse due to the lineup of the sun and planets, resulting in the loss of gravity. Computers were to crash; planes fell from the sky; gas station pumps were not to work due to electrical blackouts, and a total apocalypse was to occur. There is no science proving that the earth will lose gravity due to the lineup of planets. It never happened, yet many were so frightened that they sold everything they owned and traveled to places to pray and wait for the apocalypse. This unnecessary fear has been passed on for thousands of years.

Terrance McKenna and José Arguelles expanded the fear in the sixties when dysfunctional intellectuals believed psychedelic drugs would open the larger, unused brain power. Unfortunately, too many people bought into this lunacy, causing deaths and scars for those who lived, waking up screaming during bad dreams. Jesus warned us not to predict or to listen to those who try to predict end times.

"So, you also must be ready because the Son of Man will come at an hour when you do not expect him."

Matthew 24:44

"Of that day and hour, no one knows, not even the angels in heaven, but the Father only."

Matthew 24:36

We need to repel anyone or any news that warns of an apocalypse. God does want us to live our life feeling unnecessary fear. Scripture states that no one knows when Jesus will return and instructs us not to worry about it. If you master the book of Revelation, you will understand many other things will happen long before the apocalypse. Many, including television Christian preachers, have even tried to pinpoint dates, which is ridiculous.

One cannot use the Bible or any other books to begin calculating pinpoint dates for the beginning of the apocalypse. Several religious leaders have made a lot of money, scaring people into buying their books and audio tapes. Do not listen to any predictions, even from religious television personalities. Do not let yourself fear Apocalypse because millions have wasted time living with this fear for thousands of years.

17

I AM NEVER LUCKY

I heard so many people say, "I am never lucky." "I just don't have any luck," "If I do have luck, it is bad luck." "All that guy has is good luck; my luck is always bad." "All she touches turns to gold; I can't seem to get anything good."

They constantly complain about their luck.

However, good luck is an attitude that we can develop from how we think. God does not assign good luck to some individuals and bad luck to all others. We must think and feel lucky and good luck will follow. I do not mean good luck gambling.

Many enter the stock market without research and pick a stock like they pick a horse. "It really looks like a beautiful horse." Any system at the racetrack that you use, even looking at past performance, at the racetrack is still gambling. The stock market is for those who know what they are doing, even if they are gambling. Any uncontrollable emotion, good or bad, can change the market.

The truth is most middle- or lower-class people who enter the stock market lose money. Ask any accountant who does annual tax returns. They will tell you that most of their clients that daily trade stocks lose money in the market. If you are going to use "luck" as your reason to invest, the result will be bad luck. Even winning stocks have a bad side.

"Good luck in the stock market is often someone else's bad luck."

Matt Jordan

I know many have done well in the market. They usually are those that buy solid companies and just keep them. That is not what

18

I am talking about. I am talking about those who do it the way one would gamble, just taking chances like day traders.

I consider things like having healthy children, job success, a new home, a new car, a loving spouse, and great parents to be good luck.

No one likes to hear anyone whining about how unlucky they are. If we feel negative, negative things happen. If we feel positive, positive things happen. If we picture and believe that we see ourselves in that new car or new home, eventually, they come. However, it takes goal-setting and arduous work.

When you are doing your morning routine of prayer, meditation, prayer, and slow breathing, you then should be saying positive affirmations. "I am lucky. I am healthy. I am happy. I am successful. And, even if none of these is true, they will happen. We must keep ourselves in a lucky, positive frame of mind.

"I have had lots of luck in my career, but there has also been a lot of hard work."

Maria Sharapova

LOTTERY ADDICTION

It is a wrong decision to put off doing what we want to do in life until we win the lottery. If we want a lot of money, then we need to find a legal way to earn it. It is difficult because we first need an education in whatever we choose to do, then experience followed up with an abundance of work to receive an abundance of money. Waiting to win the lottery before we do the work that God created us to do is a huge mistake.

"He who loves money will not be satisfied with money, nor he who loves wealth... this also is vanity."

Ecclesiastes 5:10

It is true; if you are not in it, you cannot win it. But whether you buy one ticket or twenty tickets, winning the lottery is unlikely. Just look at the statistics. I just do not want anyone to postpone their dreams or their happiness until they win the lottery. Get on with your life. Do the work you love, as you will love if you choose the field of work God created you to do. Get the proper education to do it and go for it. Get the experience and then work extremely hard, and you can get anything you want in life.

Do not postpone one day of your life waiting to win the lottery. Finally, do not make bargains with God, promising what you will do if you win. Millions are praying to win the lottery. God does not choose the winner. God stays out of it.

If you must be "in it to win it," buy a ticket, but in the meantime, get on with your life and work for the things you want. Do not make it an obsession or a false idol.

"Sadly, like many times in life, including winning the lottery, we don't always get what we wish for."

Adele Rose

HUNGER FOR WEALTH

The greatest desire of many aggressive businesspersons is the desire for wealth. Financial prosperity is more important to many, more so even than seeking the kingdom of God. Just what is prosperity, and what is it not? It is vast in scope than simply how much our net worth is. There are several kinds of prosperity.

If our emotions are good and we are happy, we have good prosperity.

If we have peace in our lives, we have prosperity.

If we have God in our lives, we have prosperity.

If we are well, we have prosperity.

If we live without worry, we have prosperity.

If we have a home to live in, we have prosperity.

We have a warped sense of prosperity if we think it is just how much money we are making or have stored away.

Many drive extremely hard, all day long to get rich. However, even though money can get us things, it cannot buy us happiness. There are rich people who are unhappy and discontent, and there are poor people who are incredibly happy and content with their lives.

Becoming a "workaholic" is not good for full development. Our day must be balanced. We should work a full day, but we must leave time in the evening for the family, children's school events, hobbies, gym, and so many other things to weave in and out of lives, and so often, people seeking only wealth miss the good

21

things in life. Life should not be all work. We must take time to rest.

"He said to them, come by yourselves to a deserted place and rest for a while."

Mark 6:31

Do we try to "Keep up with the Jones?" Why? We can just share things with our neighbors and have them share with us. We are instructed to be content with what we have. We do not have to buy things that we do not need, even if they are on sale. When we go to the store, it is best to take a list of your needs.

Remember, a want without a plan is just a wish. If there are things we need or want but cannot afford at this time, we need to set up a savings plan to buy them later. Here is a great idea. Many are so consumed with trying to get rich, they do not help others. It is better to start giving some of our money to those in need instead of incessantly seeking wealth. God gives us far more back than what we give. Keep that in mind.

"It is more blessed to give than to receive."

Acts 20:30

Money is not the root of all evil; the love of money is. We can strive and work hard for all that we want if money does not become the false idle over our love of God.

We all know there is no good in trying to own the world and losing our souls. God offers us abundance, but it must be balanced with giving our family time, friends and relatives time, hobbies, sports, church and doing other things than working 24/7 to get rich at the expense of everyone else.

All the things we eventually earn are perishable. The real trophies we can take into heaven are things that we have done for

22

others. The real prize is to earn eternity in heaven, which is said to be as difficult as getting through the eye of a needle.

"Wealth consists not in having great possessions, but in having few wants."

Epictetus

DEALING WITH GREED

Webster defines greed as "a selfish and excessive desire for more of something (such as money) than is needed." You are living with or associated with someone who is greedy, selfishly wanting increasingly, and never being satisfied with what you have.

We know at this point that God wants us to be content with what we have and not covet the possessions of others. Greed can cause one to be excessively motivated and ambitious. They are hungry to get more money, never satisfied with the amount they have, even if it is the billions. More than they want money, their greed makes them want to have control over others, more than their desire for money, per se. They grasp at every chance to get more wealth. They lack restraint and covetously desire more material possessions, sometimes just to "show off" and have more than the "Joneses."

"Greed is a bottomless pit which exhausts the person in an endless effort to satisfy the need without ever reaching satisfaction."

Erich Fromm

Therefore, so many billionaires are not satisfied and keep working so hard to get more money, even if it means hurting and stealing from industrious people living paycheck to paycheck.

23

It is said that greed and narcissism both plant roots of self-doubt, creating mental disorders. This causes unhappiness because rest and calmness are not achievable at the same time, as one will not rest until their rich goals are achieved. They may even cheat or steal to get what they want. That is how bad this illness is, and I consider greed an illness one must overcome to be happy and successful. Success is not a dollar figure. It is finding out what God created us to do, getting educated on it, and then working hard to achieve it.

This greed explodes as human impulse overwhelms the constraints scripture warns us about, as they desire to gather more money, material things, and fame. Unfortunately, even though God wants us to give to the needy, those overwhelmed with greed become stingy, ignoring people in need of help.

"He who is greedy for unjust gain brings trouble on his household, but he who hates bribes will live."

Proverbs 15:27

Chapter 3

POOR CONDUCT

CONSTANT COMPLAINING

We all know people who complain all day long seemingly, never happy. They are angry at bills being too high. They complain about people who have offended them. They complain about headaches and pains. They complain about their boss being mean and unfair. They complain about friends talking about them. They complain about crooked politicians, their doctors, outside noise, and long slow lines.

They complain about not having the money to buy clothes. They complain about their church sermons being too long. They complain about prices, on and on, until they make us want to run away. Sure, many things they complain about are wrong, but no one wants to listen to someone who does nothing but complain.

The result of being an addicted complainer is that we become negative people. Other things start going wrong. It is a huge cause of going into tough times.

When someone complains all day, every day, there is a possibility that they do not know or do not accept the truth revealed in scripture.

25

"And when the people complained, it displeased the Lord."

Numbers 11:1

Do not keep friends that bring you down because they are constantly complaining. You must let any constant complaining friend know that we will always be there to assist them when they have a legitimate problem. However, we would appreciate it if they stopped complaining every time, we see them. If they do not, we need to let them find other friends who make us feel good to be around.

If we are not satisfied with what we have, it is time for us to stop complaining, set some goals that will make us happy, and get to work.

"You can be a complainer. Or you can be an achiever. But you can't be both."

Robin Sharma

PROCRASTINATION

First, we cannot ignore problems or procrastinate solving them. We all have problems, even if we are doing our best to lead a holy life. We are humans, and we all make mistakes. It is next to impossible to be perfect. However, many have more problems than others do. Why? Often, do we create our problems? When we drink too much, we will create our own problems.

When we must light up a joint every single day, we not only become brain dead, we create extra problems, not just for ourselves but for all who love us.

When we spend time with bad people who constantly do dreadful things, we will have problems. When we do something wrong, we add to our problems. When we bad mouth others, we will have problems.

I am not saying only sinful activity creates problems; people who live holy lives also have problems. We all have problems. They are a fact. I once was extremely fortunate to be at a conference where we had Norman Vincent Peale was our keynote speaker. He talked about problems. He asked us if any of us would like to hear of a place on earth where we would have no problems. Naturally, most of us raised our hands or at least said, "Yes." His answer was enormously powerful and one none of us there would ever forget. He said:

"If you would like to go someplace here on earth where you will never have to face any problems again... Just go to the nearest cemetery."

Dr. Norman Vincent Peale.

So, what can we do about problems that come up? First, thank God that we are alive and here to be able to face the problem. Second, try to enjoy solving the problem. Do some research, if necessary. Look at several alternative solutions; every problem has a solution, even if it is just the need to wait it out.

If we have a problem, we should be concerned, calm, and consider all alternatives to solve the problem.

OCCULT AND BLACK MAGIC

It is extremely dangerous to use the occult to attract love, happiness, health, success, wealth, or whatever. There are good reasons why scripture warns us to avoid the occult, black magic, witchcraft, or any evil methods to invoke the power of the devil. Some even use malicious practices to destroy someone physically, mentally, or financially. They will use a photo, hair, clothing, or other methods, all dangerous and prone to backfire. We know that whatever seeds we plant, good or bad, will come back and hit us with good luck or adverse consequences.

The occult has been practiced for numerous years. Black magic has been convoluted by people who define ritualistic practices drawing in evil spirits of the devil. Scripture warns us to avoid occultism in all forms, including fortune telling, mysticism, extra-sensory perception, parapsychology, telepathy, tarot cards, paranormal, pseudoscience, theosophy, and many others.

I believe that the various dark practices of the occult can be very damaging to both parties. The result can harm both the transmitter and the receiver. Many Psychics claim to mentally read minds and communicate telepathically through means other than their senses. There are those who incorrectly use the power to make money, and many make considerable cash, scaring people who go to them.

People gather in occult groups, casting spells upon those that they dislike. Some use voodoo dolls and sometimes stick pins in them to send their enemies pain. Many of those who practice the occult profess to believe in and love God.

I also discourage using Ouija boards because even if we think it is just a game, it can make terrible things happen to us. Many have recorded some very disturbing experiences playing this extremely dangerous game. The game draws dark forces not only to the board but also to those who play the game. Keep it away from your children. If we allow the devil into our being, he will stay there and create havoc.

When we use the occult for revenge, a price is paid, and often, it is costly. For example, they may command that someone be hurt, and that person would be hurt.

Avoid all forms of the occult.

"Reject all kinds of evil."

1 Thessalonians 5:22

It is dangerous to play with the occult, especially if we are trying to influence the mind of someone who is not interested in what we want him or her to do.

For example, we should never try to influence someone who is not interested in us to love us. For example, let us say that we become attracted to someone who has absolutely no interest in us. It is an attractive person we see at the coffee machine at work. We try to say hello and talk to them, but they give short answers and walk away. They show no interest in us, and their body language clearly tells that to us, even if they do not communicate verbally. That is their prerogative. We cannot go to a practitioner of the occult to use dark forces and liquid recipes to try to create love in that person for us.

It will backfire, haunting you, with an unbelievably bad result. It is wrong to use the occult to try to make someone love us.

Bonnie Rait sings:

"I can't make you love me if you don't. I can't make your heart feel something that it won't."

29

DANGERS OF OCCULT FRIENDS

There are several names for people practicing occultism, like spiritualists, soothsayers, fortune tellers, diviners, clairvoyants, mediums, psychics, or whatever they call themselves these days.

They are not only hurting the recipient, but they are self-inflicting pain on themselves. They are draining themselves of their energy.

"Avoid one who casts spells, psychics, mediums, or one who calls forth the spirits of the dead."

Deuteronomy 18:11

Predicting the future is wrong and in violation of God's laws. Our mind is powerful. If a psychic says something bad is going to happen, we bring it on to ourselves. This is another example of how external suggestions can be harmful to us. We should avoid idols and phenomena and get overly interested in the occult. Dark experiences begin to happen for those who practice this dangerous activity. Keep your children away from Ouija boards and violent games to help them avoid a dark and painful experience.

A clairvoyant is receiving information that no one else knows. Precognition is an advanced communication of an event that will happen in the future. We all know what tarot cards, horoscopes, and palm readings are. We should avoid these and all other occult practices because they can be dangerous when we are going to others to relate this information to us. Do we really want to know the future? Suppose they say something bad will happen? If you believe it will happen, then it will happen. Yes, we can make sad things happen that would not have occurred if we had stayed away from the occult.

It is also wrong to try to contact our loved ones who have passed on to the spiritual world.

"Do not turn to mediums or necromancers; do not seek them out, and so make yourselves unclean by them: I am the Lord your God."

Leviticus 19:31

If you feel you have something to say to someone who has entered the spiritual world, just go to a quiet place and say it. Yes, I visit my deceased loved one's graves to bring flowers on special days. Sometimes I just talk to them and hope their spirit can hear, but I do not believe that we do not have to go to a cemetery to talk to them.

Their live spirit is not there. Would you want to be? Staying in a grave site is hell.

We can talk to them from anywhere.

REACHING DISTANT LOVED ONES

We do not need to go to a psychic to reach loved ones across the country or continent. If they are ill, prayer does work. Pray for them. We should not try to read people's minds using telepathy.

God did not create us to communicate through thought or try to read another person's mind. Instead, he gave several different forms of communication. While "Telepathy" is attempting to transmit information, "Telepathic Perception" is a practice of one

31

trying to receive information from someone else's mind. Both are not accepted forms of communication in Christianity.

Quick and easy mental communication transfers such as these are wrong. We should especially never try to transmit harmful thoughts to someone. This is dangerous because the receiver did not condition the mind to receive these messages. Scripture tells us not to try to use telepathy.

"For who among men knows the thoughts of a man, except the spirit of the man which is in him?"

1 Corinthians 2:11

If we wish to communicate with a distant loved one, the best thing to do is to call or write to them. Stay away from mediums to avoid bringing the devil between you and your loved ones.

If your loved ones are sick or have a fundamental problem, you can pray for them and send them love. While I advise all who are sick to go to a doctor for a diagnosis, prayer is an important part of healing. Miracles happen every day, but we must believe.

"With God, all things are possible."

Matthew 19:26

Many distant loved ones feel that they can do nothing when a distant relative or close friend is ill, but that is not true. Be careful if you are trying to send bad wishes to anyone. This is a sin and should never be done. But, as I have said before, vengeance is God's, so knowing that should give one peace. We should never try to control the minds of others, especially those who hate us or vice versa. Remember, do not do anything inviting the devil into you because once he is in, it is difficult to get him out.

32

INTUITION IS NOT OCCULTISM

Some people practice paranormal activities, so I will define a few. Most of these are against scripture, but it is important nonetheless to understand what they are.

Telepathy is receiving information that others already know. A clairvoyant is receiving information that no one else knows. Precognition is an advanced communication of an event that will happen in the future.

However, we should listen to our intuition, *which is not* occultism. Intuition is something that comes from our own subconscious minds. We all have an intuition that we can use for our own benefit or that of our loved ones.

If we have a bad feeling about something, we should not ignore the feeling. It could be our subconscious mind warning us of something we need to be aware of or avoid. We have all heard of someone who does not get on a plane because of a bad feeling, and the plane crashes. There is nothing wrong with listening to our internal intuition; we should do so. Listen to yourself. Intuition is a beautiful thing. It is something that is occurring within us and may help us to avoid something bad. Our feelings are not to be confused with practices of occultism. They are there for us to listen to and sometimes act or avoid it for the benefit of our loved ones or ourselves.

Always keep in mind that there are two voices that try to enter our thoughts: the voice of good and the voice of evil. You just must remember the difference between right and wrong.

33

CHANGES IN PARENTS AND CHILDREN

Things have changed very much with both parents and children. Many parents do not discipline their children, and thus the children do not be afraid to do something wrong. Even God created fear; He made it clear several times in the Old Testament that He would discipline wrongful conduct, and indeed He did.

Back when I was a child, if teachers disciplined children, parents backed the teacher. The parents supported the children but gave appropriate punishments as well. Now, many parents get angry if a teacher disciplines their children. They go to the school and chastise the teacher and/or the principal. Classrooms do not have the calmness they had back when we children feared doing something wrong.

Many children are spoiled and receive sizable allowances, often without any prerequisite, such as doing the choirs or their duties. This makes children spoiled and negatively affects how they will function as adults. Dr Spock wrote that children who are not disciplined subconsciously think that they are not loved. The result is the children get worse.

Today's parents may give their teens time out and tell them to go to their rooms. So, what do the kids do? They go to their room and play on cell phones for hours, sometimes into the wee hours of the morning. I do not consider that discipline. I am not saying we should beat children. But a better disciplinary action would be to take the cell phone away for the night. The child will undoubtedly get incredibly angry, but the message will get across.

The children have changed as well. When I was a teenager, a girl whose bra strap showed, even just a piece, would be very embarrassed. Embarrassment has disappeared for many. Teen girls and many adults leave little to the imagination on a beach with thongs or whatever. Both boys and men are going to look. You cannot help but look around on packed beaches. Young boys, especially, are going to get the wrong message.

These changes in both parents and in children are not healthy, and it is one of the causes of these children going into demanding times later in life, which could have been easily prevented.

Part Two

CONQUERING HARD TIMES

Chapter 4

DEALING WITH HEALTH ISSUES

INSOMNIA

All adults spend an occasional night tossing and turning. Life is tough for all of us, and if we have a dreadful day and everything goes wrong, we take the upset to bed with us. The more we think about all the problems, aggravation from others, and things that just went wrong, the more difficult it is to go to sleep. Or we do get to sleep, but we wake up and cannot get back to sleep. If this happens every night, we will suffer from insomnia. Without taking steps to solve this torturous problem, it can cause us to move into avoidable demanding times and eventually will cause illness.

We need sleep, which restores our energy and helps us heal. We cannot go up-level in consciousness and closer to God if we are deprived of sleep. I believe all who have insomnia are extremely low in their level of consciousness. Stress levels have increased so high that we lose our self-control.

Return to the two triangles in the Introduction, and review from my first book. The charts depict the relationship between our level of consciousness and our level of power. Being down level will not only cause us to lose sleep but will negatively affect our health, happiness, and success. As we remove levels of stress, we will move up and improve health, happiness, and success.

Before we get addicted to prescription drugs to help us sleep, we need to try to work our way up level using the tools that I teach. First, I have always believed that we cannot solve any problem, including a medical problem, until we diagnose and define the core cause of the problem. Superficial pills prescribed to reduce symptoms will not solve the cause of the problem. They always have side effects we should look up before taking unless our lives depend on it. I think we should first decide what category of problems are causing our insomnia.

THINKING OF OUR "THINGS TO DO" LIST

We always have far too many things to do. This causes us to lie in bed and start thinking about them all. Then new things come to mind that we additionally must do. We begin to worry that we will forget something important, like a parent-teacher meeting or a doctor's appointment, that we forgot to write down. Often, we accumulate far too many things to do and become overwhelmed.

Learn to either say "no," or schedule it for another day.

"Do not let what you cannot do interfere with what you can do."

John Wooden

The solution to this is easy. Always keep a pen and pad by your bed on your nightstand. Take a few minutes to sit up and write the complete list. Sit and think about it for a minute because other things will come up, and you do not want to keep getting up –

especially if you are keeping a spouse awake. As soon as it is all written down, we do not have to worry about it anymore. We can relax and calm down to get the rest we need.

"...ask where the good way is and walk in it, and you will find rest for your souls."

Jeremiah 6:16

MONKEY JUMP THINKING

This is not so much a "to-do" list but a list of problems, aggravations, people who upset us, unexpected, inflated bills, children's problems, work problems, and on and on. We think of all things that make us angry, and we explode the problems, making them larger than they really are. We go through a lengthy list while "monkey jump thinking." When we are done, what do we do? We start all over and get even angrier at the people who upset us.

We are worried about some event or something else in the future. In doing so, we punish ourselves in two ways: One, we lose sleep. Two, we rob ourselves of the joy that we can feel, despite the problematic situations that we face. In many cases, it is an imagined or a possible future problem we blow out of proportion. If so, then stop thinking about it and think of something positive.

If we fail to turn off the "monkey jump" thinking, the next day we surely will be plagued with a zombie-like feeling. We will feel drowsy during the day with slowed thinking, lack energy, and feel moody.

39

Here is a little prayer that will help:

"Father God, during these exceedingly challenging times, please give me rest, peace, and joy. Let the calmness of your Spirit within me flush the pain, stress, and worry from my mind. Please bring calmness and joy to me, knowing that you live within me. Please relieve my distress and stop my mind from thinking terrible things that anger me over and over."

SICKNESS AND PAIN

It is difficult and, at times, impossible to sleep when we have sickness and pain. I have been there. Never lie awake worrying about why you feel sick. Worse yet, we should never play doctor, trying to google our symptoms to find out the illness.

Many different diseases and illnesses have the same symptoms. We are wasting our time and, in most cases, get ourselves unnecessarily worried. Getting a prompt diagnosis will lead to a solution much faster. We must go to a doctor, and get a diagnosis, even if it means getting tests, and so what we must do to get well.

FOOD AND ALCOHOL

I know people who drink coffee, energy drinks, and other caffeine products all day long and who eat a lot of sugar products and foods that turn to sugar. These will keep you awake, turn your body acidic and make you ill and cause insomnia.

Other than water and green or herbal tea, I cannot think of a single drink that is good for us other than a healthy smooth protein drink. Your first choice should always be to turn to spring water. We need to drink half of our body weight daily in water intake, which is a task. If we must have one cup of coffee a day, we need to drink it without caffeine.

LIGHT

Light affects the sleep sections of the brain and will cause insomnia for those who read in bed or use cell phones, laptops, and iPads. Keep your room dark, and you will go back to sleep. Many children stay up late, playing on cell phones, which parents should take away from them at bedtime.

We all love our children and want to be their friends. That said, there are times when we must be good parents and keep our children from harm.

MULTIPLE JOBS

I realize these troubled days, with soaring prices, many are working multiple jobs. They have no choice if they want to avoid homelessness. Just understand that working too many hours will affect your sleep and your health. Never work seven days a week. Even God rested on the seventh day, as He wanted to get us the message that we must do the same.

SERIOUS PROBLEM

Some are plagued with serious problems. Many of these have solutions, but some, although much less in number, cannot be solved. In such cases, say the Serenity prayer to help you get to the problems you cannot solve.

"God grant me the serenity to accept the things I cannot change, courage to change the things I can, and the wisdom to know the difference."

If it is a real problem that is keeping us awake, sit up for a few minutes to define the problem and list some alternative solutions that could solve them. Then prioritize those alternatives to select what you are going to do. Then turn off the light, and you will go back to sleep. If we still cannot sleep, and this has been going on for a long time, it will be necessary to find help from a friend, relative, church, expert, psychologist, or anyone who can help you. Taking some form of action is necessary at this point to stop the worry and turn it into faith.

If there is a problem you cannot solve, like the recent loss of a loved one, you need to pray that God will help you to acclimate to accepting the loss and ease the pain. This takes a long time, and I cover this much more later in the book in the segment "Loss of a Loved One." But do the exercises below to help you to get back to sleep. Words from others help truly little. But many passages in the bible will help you to resume your life.

42

"I am the resurrection and the life; he that believeth in me, though he were dead, yet shall live."

John 11:25.

The only words that will help us when we lose a loved one are the assurance that we, who believe in Jesus, will never die. Our Spirits live on eternally, and we all will get to reunite with our loved ones in heaven. In the meantime, we will find peace and give our love to our families.

If it is a solvable problem, sit up for a few minutes to define the problem. In all these different causes, be sure to do some long breathing.

"Most of the time, it is not our problem that is so bad -it is our perception of the problem."

Matt Jordan

Ask yourself, 'Just how serious is this problem?' What is the worst that can happen? Put the problem in perspective. Then list some alternative solutions that could solve them, including people that you can talk to for advice.

Then prioritize those alternatives for each problem to select what you are going to do. Then turn off the light and do the suggestions below to go back to sleep. If we still cannot sleep, and this has been going on for a long time, it will be necessary to find help from a friend, relative, church, expert, psychologist, or anyone who can help you to stop worrying, causing you to stay awake. God does not want our hearts troubled with worry.

"Therefore, I say to you, do not worry about your life."

Matthew 6:25

43

If we continue to stay awake without acting, sleep deprivation, which affects a third of the population, may occur. This dangerously affects our health. Chronic sleep deprivation can intensify the long-term risk of mental and physical health problems. We will be sleepy and drowsy the next day, which will affect our performance.

We can also experience impaired driving, lack of energy, memory lapses, slowed thinking, incisiveness, mood changes, bad decisions, stress, and anxiety.

We need anywhere between seven to nine hours of sleep. Children need more. Everyone is different. Some need fewer hours of sleep. The quality of sleep can also be a factor. We can attend a sleep lab which will help define the problem. If we sleep nine hours and do not wake up feeling refreshed, the quality of our rest may be hurt, or we may be sleeping more hours than we need. Waking up frequently to go to the bathroom will affect the overall quality of our sleep, even if we sleep eight hours. One should go to a doctor to get help if adults wake up more than once.

A sleep lab can also help us diagnose our insomnia's causes. Some with insomnia have enough time to sleep but cannot sleep. Some with sleep deprivation do not have enough time to sleep because they have not time managed their work schedule properly.

My wife and I went to a sleep specialist at our local hospital's sleep lab to help solve our problem. A sleep specialist can help determine if we have other problems like sleep Apnea, microsleeping, or an anxiety disorder. We cannot solve a problem if we do not define the core of the problem and not just treat the symptom.

Also, it is necessary to set a sleep time schedule and stick to it. We cannot "catch up on sleep" on weekends. They will just make us groggier.

OTHER TOOLS TO HELP SLEEP

BREATHE

First, take some deep breaths to try to calm down. You may have to start short and increase the length of time slowly. Begin to hold your breath in between. Again, you may have to start with short holds, but continue increasing the hold until you reach 8 or 10 seconds. Then take a deep breath and hold your breath for twenty seconds. Follow this with some quick deep short breaths. I will add a full set of various techniques for breathing.

MEDITATE

Then, meditate upon all the good promises of God.

"...meditate within your heart on your bed and be still."

Psalm 4:4

Think positive affirmations. We are the temple of God and have internal healing power. Think of any word to reduce our stress, like gentle, calm, or Jesus, my personal favorite. By the laws of Physics, this meditation has been monitored by meters and proven to reduce blood pressure, heart rate, stress levels, etc. Simply think that word over and over. At first, we will have to think the word over and over amazingly fast to avoid our troublesome thinking returning. However, it will slow down in time as we release stress and calm down.

45

PRAY

Pray for help. God lives within us, so we have God much closer to hear your prayers. It is like we have our own God. This is a great answer if someone asks you, "How can God hear all the millions of prayers that are going on constantly?

"The Lord himself goes before you and will be with you. He will never leave you nor forsake you. Do not be afraid; do not be discouraged."

Deuteronomy 31:8

READ

If nothing above works, sit up and read the bible. Just open it up and trust God to send you to the right section. Or just go to proverbs. But God will listen to you and bring you comfort so that you may sleep.

Lean on God in the quiet night during sleeplessness and trust in his words. You will grow tired. If you are not reading the bible, be sure you are reading a relaxing book. When we get tired from reading, we go back down and start breathing and tools above again.

THOUGHT CONTROL

While lying awake and thinking a bunch of annoying things, we must shut off the thinking. Try taking a deep breath and holding it for 20 seconds. Then count backward from 100 to 0.

If that does not work, strongly think of the words: "shut up" over and over. While you are thinking this, think like you are yelling and commanding your brain to stop thinking out of control. When this happens to me, I do this, and it works.

If none of this helps, we need to decide who can best help. This is a genuine problem that can affect our life. We may need a doctor or sleep specialist to help us define our problem(s), especially if we cannot solve it using the suggestions above.

Do not let it continue. Do something.

Your life depends on it.

"The best bridge between despair and hope is a good night's sleep."

E. Joseph Cossman

ANXIETY AND PANIC ATTACKS

"Anxiety does not empty tomorrow of its sorrows, but only empties today of its strength."

Charles Spurgeon

To prevent anxiety from zapping our strength, we must take strong action to overcome it. We should start by ruling out the possibility that we have Generalized Anxiety Disorder, or GAD, is a mental illness. Those with GAD worry much more often than the majority. Anxiety is sometimes caused by a mental or physical condition, prescription or illegal drugs, excess stress, or a physical condition. The doctor's initial task is to see if your anxiety is a symptom of another medical condition.

Anxiety causes us to feel an intense wave of fear, immobilizing our ability to deal with situations. We may sweat, feel extreme fatigue, and our heart pounds. It becomes difficult to breathe, and we may even perceive that we are losing our minds - or worse yet, feel like we are dying. We often become so anxious that we take our anxiety out of proportion to whatever caused the anxiety.

During periods of anxiety, our mind craves peace, relaxation, quiet, and escape from the place or situation that is causing the anxiety. It is during these periods that scripture advises us to break away.

"Come aside... rest a while."

Mark 6:31

This will help us to avoid exploding the problem because it can lead to intense anxiety and mental breakdown. When we feel anxious, we first should stop what we are doing, rest, and take at least some deep breaths until we feel a sense of calmness. After a few breaths, hold your breath for a 20 to 30 count. Then push it out through your mouth. After we do the breathing, we must begin thinking positive thoughts, like:

"I will overcome this."

"I will not let my heart be troubled." (John 14:1)

"I can do all things through Christ that strengthen me," (Philippians 4:13)

"This situation can be solved."

"I must collect myself and control my thoughts."

"I am lucky to be alive."

"I will control this anxiety."

"I know I can overcome this."

"Why am I worrying when most things we worry about never happen?"

Say each of these three times and believe each with all your heart. Make up a few of your own.

A panic attack hits without notice. When it hits, we must take some fast, and then long, breaths. Then, again take a long breath and hold it for at least 20 seconds.

Then we need to count backward from 100 to 0. Do these as often as necessary.

Usually, there does not exist real danger, unless we are thinking about suicide - and that is when we must seek immediate help.

49

When we suffer from anxiety, our worries explode many times over. We could become so emotionally out of control; we cannot function normally with day-to-day responsibilities. The demands of life just are overwhelming. Many cannot get out of bed. If that happens, turn to God for comfort.

"I will both lie down, in peace, and sleep; for You alone, O Lord, make me dwell in safety."

Psalm 4:8.

When we feel some peace and quiet, we should analyze whether the trigger was real or an exaggerated problem that we took out of proportion. Now that we understand the problem, we can put it in perspective. In a way, we have failed to heed God's warning to "Be anxious for nothing." We must learn to live life effectively, without anxiety while doing the things we must do during our daily activities.

Of course, we should never watch, nor allow our children to watch, horror or violent movies because they will increase our anxiety and are bad for us anyway.

Instead, put on some relaxing music, especially Christian music. Or put on YouTube relaxation videos. If you have Alexa, ask her to play "Liquid Mind," and the sound of ambient music will calm you. If you are sitting or lying down, look for things to look at, like ocean scenes, deep water fish, or nighttime boat light parades.

My dad once said to me when I was a child, "Mental pain can feel worse than physical pain." He had a nervous breakdown and he had to stay in bed for a couple of weeks. Many professionals say, "there is no such thing as a nervous breakdown." That is because they cannot find the science behind it.

I say that they are wrong because I have experienced it, and so have both my mom and dad. A nervous breakdown is real. Use the tools in this book to get back to normal. We allow intense anxiety and panic attacks to accumulate over time – in the end, it leads to us becoming unable to cope with life. We cannot function, and many become bedridden.

PSYCHOSOMATIC ILLNESS

The word psychosomatic means a person who feels like they have a health problem, but a doctor cannot diagnose a medical condition. The person that has these feelings may be overly concerned about the symptoms that they feel to the point that they cannot function.

We all watched old movies and heard a doctor, who found nothing wrong with a patient, say they gave them "sugar pills," containing no medicine, and guess what? They felt better. They did not heal anything in the body, but they had them thinking they took something that would heal them.

The idea that our brain can convince our body to heal with a fake treatment is real and called the placebo effect. Placebo healing has been around for millennia. However, science has found that under the right circumstances, a placebo can be just as effective as traditional treatments.

"The placebo effect is more than positive thinking. It can make someone think they are sick or believe that a fake treatment will work. It is about creating a stronger connection between the brain and body and how they work together," said Professor Ted

Kaptchuk of Harvard-affiliated Beth Israel Deaconess Medical Center, whose research focuses on the placebo effect.

Placebos will not lower cholesterol or shrink a tumor; instead, placebos work on symptoms modulated by the brain, like the perception of pain. "Placebos may make you feel better, but they will not cure you," says Kaptchuk. "They have been shown to be most effective for conditions like pain management, stress-related insomnia, and cancer treatment side effects like fatigue and nausea."

For many years, the medical industry considered placebos a sign of failure. A placebo is used in clinical trials to evaluate the effectiveness of treatments and is most often used in drug studies. For instance, people in one group get the actual drug, while the others receive an inactive drug or placebo. The participants in the clinical trial do not know if they receive the real thing or the placebo. Researchers can measure if the drug works by comparing how the groups react, one with medicine and the other without. If they both have the same reaction, with or without any improvement, they consider the drug simply did not work.

Many people who are not sick end up imagining the symptoms of a real illness. They are deceiving themselves. The consequences of this can be the self-development of real illnesses.

*"Do not be deceived, God is not mocked; for whatever a man
sows, that he will also reap."*

Galatians 6:7

If we continue to deceive ourselves, believing we are ill, even
if we are not, we are planting the wrong seeds. Real sickness will
come upon us. Your mind can be a powerful self-infliction cause
of an illness.

Of course, there are people with real illnesses that should go to
a doctor when feeling sick. I do believe we should take all the tests
to get a diagnosis. I further believe that in many cases, we can find
natural ways to heal at an alternative doctor, but if we do not find
them, of course, we must take the prescribed medicine.

*"Fear ordinarily does not lead to illness if the organism can
flee successfully. If the individual cannot flee but is forced to
remain in a conflict situation which cannot be resolved, fear may
turn into anxiety and psychosomatic changes may then
accompany anxiety."*

Rollo May

HYPOCHONDRIA

Hypochondria is like a psychosomatic condition, with a slight
difference. People with Hypochondria create a disproportionate
problem in the sense that a small symptom may seem huge to them.
Those that have a psychosomatic condition create high anxiety,
making them feel that the symptoms are stopping them from
functioning normally.

Often, we hear hypochondriacs say that they are sick all the time. Each time they give you a list of ailments, some repeats and some new. Due to their condition, they end up magnifying all their illnesses to an absurd degree.

They continue to say they feel anxiety due to the sickness they feel, even though in many instances, they have developed a Nocebo, a psychosomatically created illness. Even a simple sneeze from pollen can convince someone with Hypochondria that they have a serious and terrible disease. They get up every day and go to work. They seem to function, yet they believe they are extremely sick; in truth, however, they suffer from Hypochondria. They react negatively when told that there is nothing medically wrong with them, even after being evaluated by doctors for every illness.

If I am approached, I advise them to find a good bible-based church. God can and wants to help.

"The Lord sustains them on their sickbed and restores them from their bed of illness."

Psalm 41:3

I know several Christians who are the opposite of a Hypochondriac. When someone talks about sickness, they say, "I do not get sick." They believe that God wants us to be happy and healthy. They stay positive. They eat healthy, exercise, stay in touch with God, take supplements, rest, and live healthy lives. They do not get sick. They may get an injury or a cold, but they shake it off and will it away. We are the temple of God whose Spirit leaves within each of us. With this, we have the inner healing power to heal many illnesses by willing them away in the name of Jesus.

In all cases, I strongly urge anyone who feels sick to go to a doctor for medical tests and a diagnosis and do whatever they must do to get healed.

54

Whether one is suffering from a psychosomatic or hypochondriac condition, they are unnecessarily traveling into hard, avoidable tough times. They need to get help, get a medical diagnosis, and put their health problems in perspective. Only then can they be healed; however, their refusal to do so makes one wonder if they enjoy complaining about their health.

When someone asks, "How are you," do they really want to hear a list of complaints? "Hello" makes much more sense to me.

DEPRESSION

Depression is a mood ailment that causes a constant feeling of sadness and loss of interest in activities. This also would include things that they used to love in their lives.

It is a wretched disorder that affects how we think, feel, and behave. It can lead to a variety of emotional and physical problems in behavior. Fortunately, it is also treatable. In mild cases, one can go to a church for help or several other organizations that can help.

If it is a clinical depression, it will require assistance from a psychiatrist, as a prescription will be needed along with psychiatric care. If not clinical, then a psychologist is suggested to attend therapy. One can determine if it is clinical by getting a "screening" from a psychiatrist. Other symptoms may include trouble sleeping, appetite changes, fatigue, loss of energy, feeling guilty, difficulty concentrating and, more seriously, suicidal thoughts. Instances of self-harm, with or without a knife, may also occur.

Medical conditions such as depression can also be symptoms of a brain tumor, thyroid problems, or vitamin deficiency, so it is important to rule out general medical causes. So, it is an innovative idea to do this, if possible, before trying a psychologist. If the doctor and the philologist both eliminate their plausible causes, a psychiatrist will have to perform a screening that may show a chemical imbalance. While I always would rule out all-natural healing methods before I turn to medical prescriptions, medicine usually is required to heal a chemical imbalance.

Almost 7% of the population is diagnosed with depression each year in the United States, and about 17% of the population will experience depression at some time in their life. Depression can occur at any time but usually appears during the late teens to mid-twenties. Women are more likely than men to experience depression. Some studies show that one-third of women will experience a major depressive episode in their lifetime. About 40% of people who inherit genes making them susceptible to depression are eventually subjected to it.

The Devil loves for us to be depressed and will do all he can to make us unhappy. Living in his world is a life of depression. Depression can result in a life away from God and his Bible – a life lived in a hell of overthinking and wrongdoings. The armies of the devil work hard, hammering us with lies that can drive us into depression. Their goal is for those suffering to commit suicide, a choice no one should ever make.

In my first book, I explain why we feel bad – because of dropping down in our level of consciousness. Stress causes this. Wrongful conduct causes stress. Listening to the wrong messages on television or the news can cause depression. Friends who feed us negativity can cause depression.

We must learn how to feel joy, regardless of the disasters and negative events in the world. We can find that joy by keeping our love for Jesus deep within ourselves.

Depression will cause many other problems and certainly will take us into unnecessarily tough times. However, it can be cured. There is hope. One should always seek help and not let this painful condition ruin their life.

FACING A SERIOUS OPERATION

The most difficult serious operation I ever had to face was a quad-bypass heart surgery. I began to get out of breath easily, going up steps or walking up a hill. It got so bad that I had to sit down and rest before I could keep going. Those that never had one have no idea how scary the thought is of having someone open your chest, move the lungs, and start cutting arteries. I was scared – very scared. I did not want to go through with it, but with the blood flow completely closed, there was no alternative.

After various tests, the first heart doctor told me I had to go through with it, so I went to both a second heart doctor and my natural doctor for an opinion. The tests revealed that I needed a quad bypass. It is urgent to select a surgeon with great credentials and many good references for their "bedside manner."

"It is the surgeon's duty to tranquilize the temper, to beget cheerfulness, and to impart confidence of recovery."

Astley Cooper

I selected the second surgeon I met at the Cornell Presbyterian hospital in New York City. The doctor said that I was extraordinarily strong when he looked at all my tests and examined

57

me. He said that I would do very well. Fortunately, I have been going to the gym all my life, ever since I graduated college.

Of course, I wanted to meet the anesthesiologist, as he or she is so critical to the surgery. I asked him and my doctor a large list of my questions – as you should when facing any surgery. I wanted to know not just what happens during surgery but also what I could expect after the procedure. I asked the anesthesiologist what would happen if I woke during the surgery. He said he would be present, constantly monitoring, and that would not happen.

I prepared myself mentally, using positive affirmations and relaxation techniques I had taught many others to use. I set my mind to be positive, understanding the medications for pain, and visualizing myself quickly step-marching again with the Ohio State University marching band.

When I got on the operating table, I did all I could to be convinced this was necessary. I chose the right medical team and hospital, understood everything, and was not scared at all. I felt confident because I knew I did all that I could and was highly confident all would be successful. I cracked jokes and made everyone laugh. I knew God would protect me with angels in the room.

"So do not fear, for I am with you; do not be dismayed, for I am your God. I will strengthen you and help you."

Isaiah 41:10

In this, I felt confident that it would be a success and that I would fully recover – though that took over a year. But I did recover. I even marched several times at games and the tours we did with the band to France and elsewhere. Life returned to normal.

58

THE DANGER OF CELL PHONES

Many do not know that cell phones are extremely dangerous to our bodies. The radiation, especially on high radiation 5G, can cause serious illness. If you buy a case that straps to your body, know that this is dangerous. Turn the phone off when the phone is in the case or anywhere on your body. Cell phones that are on make us vulnerable to radiation absorption. Of course, some websites dispute this, but who do you think created these websites? EMF's (Electromagnetic frequencies) are harmful to the body.

Find the websites that explain this. You do not have to believe my opinion. Then get Kinesiology assessed and see for yourself how the cell phone weakens your body. Kinesiology is the science of testing items against the body to find out whether your body accepts or rejects them. Some call this a "muscle test," but it is the science of Kinesiology.

Set your cell phone to be used only with Bluetooth in your car. If your car does not have that capability, get a holder you can attach to your dashboard and keep the phone in that.

This is serious. Do not just quickly read this and move on. Many of us already have illnesses due to cell phones, known or unknown. There are those that have long, one-hour conversations using a cell phone held to their head. There have even been cases of tumors growing in the head due to cell phones being held to the ear. There are many using the old "flip-phones" due to the dangers of radiation emitted from later-generation cell phones. 5G emits the heaviest radiation of all past generations.

I highly suggest that everyone get a landline for telephone conversations. I realize that many got rid of their landlines when they got cell phones to save money. However, you can find landlines available for as low as $10 a month. Whatever the costs are, they are certainly cheaper than a serious illness. Then, when someone calls your cell, tell them to call your landline if the conversation is longer than a few seconds. Or have them call you back, so they know to always call your landline first. Any use of a cell phone should be on the speaker phone. Avoid all contact with your body.

What does this have to do with this book? Everything. My goal is to help people understand, conquer, and avoid tough times. Illness from unsafe cell phone use can bring you ridiculously tough times. Yes, that could take a long time to occur, but why gamble with your life?

I AM TIRED ALL THE TIME

I speak from experience. I used to say this all the time, and guess what? During that period of my life, I was tired all the time. Our body will feel as we think, good or bad. There are a lot of real reasons we can feel tired. Over time, fatigue gets worse and worse until it overcomes us. We continue to keep ourselves in this state of weakness for days, even weeks. We slowly begin to break down our immune system. Our health breaks down.

We become overwhelmed. It is time to stop everything to rest when we feel so exhausted. We are a nervous wreck and feel like we are having a nervous breakdown. While in a low level of consciousness and being highly stressed, we cannot function efficiently in our jobs, businesses, or tasks. Our happiness turns into sadness, our success into failure, and our health into illness. We must stop what we are doing and calm down.

60

"Then, because so many people were coming and going that they did not even have a chance to eat, he said to them, "Come with me by yourselves to a quiet place and get some rest."

Mark 6:31

Even God, after creating the heavens and all on earth in six days, rested on the seventh day. He wanted to set an example. He certainly did not need the rest. But He warned that we all need at least one day a week rest, or we begin to break down.

However, there are physical and mental reasons which also can cause fatigue. We should go to our primary doctor for a physical and a prescription for a full series of blood tests. Our doctor may also refer us to a specialty doctor or a sleep lab on a follow-up visit. Certainly, a lack of quality sleep will cause fatigue the next day.

If we exhaust all medical possibilities, we may need to look for a mental problem that can exhaust anyone. I always recommend a psychologist first. If you cannot get a solution there, then see a psychiatrist.

We should also be sure to do our morning routine to reduce stress and rise in consciousness and available inner power. Repeating positive affirmations can also help.

Do not accept people telling you there is nothing wrong. If you feel tired, something is wrong.

Finally, if we are in the senior generation, people, including doctors, will say, "You are old. You must be tired." I hate this. You do not. If you explore all the top and find nothing, take a nap.

"Mental illness and chronic fatigue are comparable to a dead soul inhabiting a surviving body."

Steven Magee

61

WEIGHT PROBLEM

Many overweight people around the world would love to lose weight. Weight loss is a billion-dollar business. Some are heavy due to a medical or metabolism issue. No doubt, when we are teased or see ourselves in the mirror as overweight, we may lose self-esteem. I have seen many overweight people who changed their diet and lost many unneeded pounds. Why do we overeat?

"Well, I think probably the reason most people overeat is stress."

Jenny Craig

Often, when we feel stressed, we tend to want to do things like eat a lot of snacks, most of which are bad for us. The body creates fat cells to protect, leading to being overweight. We all must learn to eat foods that are good for us and restrain ourselves, at least most of the time, from foods known to be bad for us.

We all know the foods that are bad for us. For my book, "Unleash Godly Power," I researched for several years the reasons why we get sick. I listed many foods that are bad for us. We all know about fatty meat, processed meat, trans fats, junk fast foods, chemicals in non-organic foods, or sugar. I listed acidic foods that drop our pH rate and healthy foods that bring the body to a healthier alkaline pH.

Giving harmful foods up is hard to do. We crave the things that are bad for us. Did you ever crave tofu or sprouts? It seems that most foods that taste good and those that do not taste favorable are good for us. The body develops fat to protect us from the bad foods we ingest. The body produces fat cells to protect us. The more

62

acidic foods we eat, the heavier the body will become, and it does not stop growing.

Many people are overweight due to eating too much food. Every now and then, we must lose that extra five pounds we put on, especially on holidays. We do not have to go hungry to lose weight. We must give up carbohydrates like bread, pizza and pasta and focus on healthy organic alkaline salads and vegetables. If you get the right recipes and cook these properly, these foods can and do taste delicious.

I will warn everyone that vegetables fried in hot oil are carcinogenic. Most snacks are also extremely dangerous and will cause weight gain. Instead of eating potato chips, candy, and things bad for us, we should snack on foods that are good for us. Go to a health food store and look in their snacks isle and you will find numerous healthy snacks.

We do temporary diets for a few weeks but losing some weight and returning to our old eating habits is a waste of time. The body will send food to protect itself, and the weight will quickly return. Why roller coaster your weight up and down when you can change your eating habits and keep the weight off? Consider beyond meat alternatives that taste like meat. Yes, if you do enough research, you can eat a healthy sausage and pepper sandwich that tastes great and many other beyond-meat alternatives. I believe a small amount of low-fat, organic meats like fillet mignon can be good for us and help prevent anemia.

The other benefit of eating a lot of alkaline foods is they help to prevent cancer, parasites, and many illnesses. Most of these diseases thrive in an acidic body and cannot survive in an alkaline body. Do some research and make a list of acidic foods and drinks to avoid and a list of alkaline foods to eat. As far as things to drink, water should be the vast majority of what we drink. Organic green

63

tea and some herbal teas can be healthy and even healing. Scripture advises us not to be gluttons of eating.

"The one who keeps the law is a son with understanding, but a companion of gluttons shames his father."

Proverbs 28:7

ABORTION PTSD

Many have experienced an abortion either personally or with regard to a relative, friend, or spouse. Indeed, fathers may also be an equal part of an abortion, alongside women. Many women, and even some men, suffer from "Post Traumatic Syndrome" deeply after, often regretting the act. They wonder, *will God forgive us?*

Many Christians wonder about this. Will God forgive us for violating His law? Yes, God forgives all the mistakes when we are born again. Jesus died on the cross to forgive all sins when we were born again, accepting Jesus as our Lord and Savior. Nonetheless, He expects us to do the right thing in the future.

However, those of us who are "pro-life," believe an unexpected, unwanted child can have a fruitful life after being adopted by loving new parents. Many are lined up, waiting for the baby to adapt to raise, live and enjoy. The argument is not about a woman's right to do as she wishes with her body. It is about whether the child has a right to live. Most Christians support "pro-life" and advise those considering an abortion to allow the child to live and put it up for adaption.

Science is not always correct, tainted at times by evil people who have their own agenda of controlling the population and

64

money. They argue that a fetus is not a baby. Scientists try to make the argument that the fetus is like a parasite and is not a child yet. But the truth is that a fetus is the start of a child, created by God to grow, develop, and be born to a life to be lived to the fullest.

However, if the mistake was made in the past, nothing can be done to turn it around. All those who made a mistake and suffered from depression or remorse due to its need to understand that they have been forgiven. It is time to get over it and move on. We cannot allow it to affect us for the rest of our lives. When we become born again, our Spirit is not only perfect but we are forgiven for all sins, not some sins, all sins.

Both the father and the mother must take responsibility for what they think is a mistake. The man is equally responsible, especially if he pays and/or drives the mother to the place of abortion. Any man who blames the mother and does not own up to doing the right thing is not only wrong but a coward. Man up and do the right thing. Take a share of the responsibility. Look into adoption. Have discussions with your mate. Be supportive and help her to decide. I have zero respect for a man who just walks away.

"Your eyes saw my unformed body; all the days ordained for me were written in your book before one of them came to be."

Psalms 139:16

65

WE BUILD A NEW HEALTHY BODY

The good news is that our cells continuously replace themselves. Scientists have said that we periodically grow all new cells and a new body. They disagree on how long this takes, saying that it can take anywhere from eleven months to eleven years. We can shorten the period by absorbing all the advice I share in the health section later in the book. Even in the longer period, it is wonderful to know we can be new again.

However, we decide if we are getting new and healthy cells. If we or someone else has planted in our minds that we will have a health defect all our lives, our subconscious will accept that, and we will fail to replace cells with new, vibrant, and healthy ones. Unfortunately, some people are handicapped and cannot get themselves in an elevated level of available godly power; the fact saddens me, as I would love to see everyone healed.

Disease and sickness are unnatural and should not occur. If we fall into the false premise that we will always be sick, we will always be sick. We will fail to accept new healthy cells and a chance to start all over again with a healthy body. I am not saying that we can live forever. We all know that we must die sometime. However, I passionately believe that we all can live to ripe, incredibly old ages with good health and many more years than the average person in this age.

It is said that great empires died when growth terminated. The same can be said for our bodies. Too many people tell themselves, "I am getting old," so guess what? They get old.

"The cells of your body aren't old, they keep regenerating, they are new. Your body has the potential of being as young and as vital as it has ever been, you see… You don't have old cells; you just have an old attitude about your new self."

Abraham Hicks

Chapter 5

PERSONAL PROBLEMS

MY SPOUSE BEATS ME

If you are a battered woman, common sense should tell you that you will never find happiness until you get out!

If Freedom lies between love and happiness, then you know which choice to make because it does not matter if you think you love your spouse or boyfriend.

In the end, fear is most probably what holds you from truly peeling yourself away from them. You may not love him and are simply too scared to get out, but you will not start healing until you make that leap of faith.

Love and Happiness can heal; faster than you may think. You must have heard the saying, 'If you love something, set it free.' If the monster does not love you or give you the respect you deserve, then you must respect yourself enough to leave them so that you may grow.

You will forget that you ever loved the monster. Any man who hits a woman is a monster and does not deserve your love or attention.

A battered wife or girlfriend must unleash herself permanently from the prison of her own making. No matter what they promise you, they will hit you again. Heed my words, the moment you experience your partner's aggression, and he has raised a hand against you, warn your loved ones. Find safety and ensure that it does not happen again and that you will leave if it does.

Be firm about protecting your life and spirit. You can only forgive this terrible act one time. In certain cases, if you think it will never repeat itself as you know the man well enough, then chances are you will not because monsters hide in sheep's clothing.

Please, protect yourself and get out.

You are a fool for enduring a single slap, let alone a full beating. I was on a grand jury and could not believe how many men went to jail for beating up their wives. Some would even slash them with knives.

We heard prison-recorded conversations about the girl telling the man in jail how much she loves and misses the demon. No one could understand why the girls would even take the calls. The men only called to tell them they were sorry and only did so because they wanted to threaten them not to testify in court. They did all they could to make the girls think that they had caused the beating, which was unbelievable.

Today we call this behavior *gaslighting,* where the victim is made to believe that they deserved the treatment or had created the roof of the problem that needed rectifying. Any man who beats a woman is mentally disturbed. Stand up to him and hang in there, have faith that the situation will douse itself if you are holding the pot of water. Never allow the fire to burn you; tell him very clearly that you are not taking it anymore.

Tell him he will be behind bars if he ever tries to see you again because you will get an "order of protection" from the authorities.

69

If you are threatened, call the police immediately. Call the police or social services to ask for advice if you are too scared, and if you cannot, then do not fret. Some organizations will help you to get out of that situation. You do not have to do it alone. Failure to do something could even result in your death, or near death, and scar any children involved for life.

I realize it is difficult to leave, especially if you have children. However, realize that even if they are in another room, they hear all this. Closed doors do not block sound. It scares and mentally scars the children for life. They develop inhibitions about relationships; some grow up just to abuse their spouses or children.

It is not good to keep children in a dysfunctional home; you are doing them a great injustice by staying there. I have seen children come into court, crying to testify on behalf of their moms. In some cases, the man hit the kids too. One held his son in front of him with a knife to his neck. An abused woman can avoid situations like this if they act much sooner, thus not only saving the futures of their children but also avoiding damage to their mental health.

If you are scared, as most women in that situation are, pray to God and ask for strength to make problematic decisions.

"Whenever I am afraid, I will trust in You."

Psalm 56:3

If you are someone who knows of an abused woman, you need to report it, even if it means the end of your friendship. You know about the beatings. When you hear excuses like, "I fell down the steps," or "I ran into a door," you know they are not telling you the truth, especially if you have seen these bruises more than once.

"At any given moment, you have the power to say, 'This is not how the story is going to end.'"

Christine Mason Miller

PROBLEMATIC DAYS

We all have had the feeling that everything we are doing within the day goes wrong.

We complain, and others add to it by saying, "It never rains unless it pours." If so, does this happen day after day? We all go through rugged roads, but something is wrong when this happens continuously. Some paths we take will be rough, boring, rugged, and tedious.

Life is like a coin. We have heads and tails. Therein, there is a duality of harmony and chaos present. Some days will be filled with problems related to our jobs, health, marriage, relationships, disobedient children, bills, estranged close relatives, and the list will go on with our life.

But sometimes, we all have a day when absolutely nothing goes right. We drop things all day long, miss most lights, cut ourselves in the kitchen, a child gets hurt or is in trouble, our computers break down, we feel lousy, someone calls to criticize us, and so on and so on. In all cases of our insomnia, we must stop thinking and take some slow long deep breaths.

The truth is this. Great sailors are not made to navigate smooth oceans and seas. It is rocky times and storms that mold them into better strength, character, expertise, and success. Smooth, calm

71

waters are just a way of coasting and relaxing. They do not grow from them. Nor do we grow from a day everything seems to go right, not that we have days like that often.

But keep in mind what scripture has to say.

"Let not your heart be troubled."

John 14:1

We need to learn from problematic days and grow from them. Perhaps analyzing what could we have done differently to have had a better day? We must stop, take long breaths, and meditate on our day. We are supposed to stay in control and let bad days get the better of us.

Meditate and breathe to calm down. We will face delays, sometimes in high traffic, or stop for a prolonged period for construction, waiting over an hour for a doctor who is way behind schedule, whatever. We can either steam and sit there swearing and shifting around in anger, turn a negative into a positive and meditate while waiting to reduce stress and enjoy the day or get angry over it.

Sometimes, we need to realize that some things are out of our control; therefore, we need to turn our attention to ourselves because we know that we can walk away from the source of chaos to find harmony. Instead of building stress and lowering our level of power, we can use delay periods to rise consciousness while reducing stress instead of adding stress which drops our level of consciousness and reduces our power and energy.

"Consider it pure joy whenever you face trials of many kinds because you know that the testing of your faith produces perseverance."

James 1:2-3

72

Turning problematic days into happy days starts with how and what we are thinking. As I always say, "Find a way to turn a negative into a positive."

Humans have acute senses, and we feel what we think. I realize many will say, "This is easier said than done," and you are right. Sometimes it is extremely tough to do, which means fighting your thoughts, over and over, until you change and win. Whenever problems are getting us down, we should look up. We can do all things with God on our side. He is always there, ready, willing, and able.

"We must go through many hardships to enter the kingdom of God."

Acts 14:22

I LOST THE LOVE OF MY LIFE

Losing a spouse is like losing half of our body. I cannot imagine losing mine. The Lord gifts us with our better half; losing such a gift can rip our hearts apart.

But should this emotion be reserved for our romantic partners? Losing a parent, child, or even a sibling is also very painful. I know words do not help a victim when in a state of grief, but some blurt words like, "He is better off." "She has no pain now." "He is in a better place."

Instead of imparting hollow condolences, sharing silence and your company with a grieving individual is sometimes appropriate. It is better to sit by your relative or friend who lost a loved one, hold their hand, and be there for them. One that annoys me is, "Let me know if there is anything I can do to help."

Do not speak about your aid, help them without words. Do not make statements because people suffering from such pain will not think to call you for help. They are preoccupied with a form of pain that shrouds them like a winter fog; only you can be the beacon of light that can call them home.

Without a word, check up on them. Make a plate of food and bring it over, call them from time to time but ensure that you allow them the space to grieve properly.

It is important to remember that God created the emotions of grief; therefore, the act of weeping makes us feel better by unleashing our pain physically without harming anyone. Holding it in, as I have seen others do, is to postpone healing and to acclimate to the loss.

Some wait months or even years to let the tears roll out. Holding it in can scar you for life if you do not release the pent-up emotions you feel. Some final cry about it, years later. There is no reason to wait. When we withhold grief, it will have a negative impact on us both physically and emotionally. This can result in insomnia, headaches, stomach, and other problems.

The tears wash away the sadness, and we get the deeply inbred grief out. Some sob uncontrollably, losing the power of emotional responses. But they are getting the grief out, and that is a good thing. Let them go.

Unfortunately, men especially, feel that adults should not cry. Nothing can be farther from the truth. Those that hold it in have serious effects on their daily living. They are not themselves. How long does it take to get over it? The length of time it takes is different for individuals. The ones you love the most will take the longest. The most important message to get through to a grieving person is this:

"Very truly, I tell you, the one who believes has eternal life."

John 6:47

We must remember that although our body will do, our soul lives on. If we are in the Lord, death becomes a celebration of life, a continuance of life.

A life in heaven is so amazing. Toward the end of this book, I will present my studies on just what heaven will look like. Keeping this in mind will help those who lose someone close to them know that you will reunite one day for eternity. Scripture states that all who believe in Jesus will go to heaven, as all sins are forgiven.

We need to turn to God to reduce suffering.

"Our hope for you is steadfast because we know that you are partakers of the suffering, so also you will be of the consolation"

2 Corinthians 1:7

Our lost loved ones are welcome in the arms of Jesus. The apostle Paul affirmed that those who believe in Jesus do not have to grieve. Paul advises that the second coming of Jesus will reunite those of us alive with those who have passed.

"For we believe that Jesus died and rose again, and so we believe that God will bring with Jesus those who have fallen asleep in Him. .... We who are still alive and are left will be caught up together with them in the clouds to meet the Lord in the air. And so, we will be with the Lord forever. Therefore, encourage one another with these words."

Thessalonian 4: 13-18

75

A TIME NOT TO BE HAPPY

We cannot always be happy because, with times of happiness, there will come times of grief to evaluate our determination and faith in this lifetime.

There is a time for everything, but we must choose wisely.

For example, one of the things I hate most is going to a wake and hearing people laughing. I understand that we run into people we have not seen for a long time. It is natural to want to catch up on old times. However, laughing at a wake disrespects the deceased person and those in tears from witnessing an event of great sadness.

When you have met people from times past, some people lost their loved ones for all eternity. One can catch up after the wake and funeral.

There is a time and a place for everything, and there are times it is respectful to refrain and to show respect. It just takes some common sense and discretion to understand what conduct is appropriate during a situation we are in, especially at a funeral.

If we genuinely love the person we lost or their loved ones, we should respect them. Reverence is an important segment of love. Sometimes we must show that love by hugging someone or by holding their hand. Friends and relatives, who love each other, not only laugh together but also cry together.

We should get them laughing together after the funeral, at the usual get-together most families have.

It is possible that the deceased's spirit may be present at the wake. It has been said that the Spirit hangs around after death for

76

a while. So, if the spirit is present, would he or she be happy hearing people laughing at their funeral?

That even at the time of their death, nobody remembers them fondly. It is a solemn and sad event. People who hold utmost respect and love for the deceased are mourning, not laughing. When I was at a wake after losing a loved one, I cried and was not incredibly happy listening to a few people laughing.

Therefore, remember that before you see someone that you wish to laugh with at a wake, imagine how you would feel if you lost a loved one. I do pray that such a situation never befalls a person but please, have some respect.

I CAN NOT FIND A SPOUSE

While I think we must look nice and neat, we should try to be ourselves, especially to people that we try to impress.

We should speak the truth and not slant it in any way when we first talk to a potential spouse. They are sizing us up as we are doing the same to them. Most importantly, we need to investigate the other person's heart more so than the body.

We need to understand that our bodies will always be subject to change. If people desire a fit person, they need to understand that they can adopt exercise and diet plans with a person they love thus, create a healthy habit that the couple can enjoy!

Hence, if you find someone whose personality you love but do not like the way they look, then it can be changed, but please, do not place vanity on top of a pedestal. Realize if you are judging someone for faults, they are doing the same to you.

Find a space for genuine honesty for a person's disposition within your heart. Women do not have to turn into cover models, and men do not have to look like male models.

We need to get into conversation and investigate the heart. Looks and bodies will change as we age, but our hearts will remain the same. Why should it be what we are looking for? Divorce is exceedingly high among marriages established with vain hearts. Appearance is not what the Lord is looking for so when he judges us.

"The Lord looks at the heart."

Samuel 16:7

Keep in mind that we must love before we can be loved. Show love and compassion for everyone. Remember, love is not controllable. We cannot force ourselves to love someone, and we cannot force others to love us.

But when you find that special one and they have found you, you will both know it because you will feel it. Be patient, and do not try to force it. God will send you His help and the best mate for you.

Ask God to help.

"...whatever you ask in my name, the Father will give you. This is my command; Love each other."

John 15:16-17

Before we give our heart to someone else, we must find out where their heart is. The biggest cause of divorce is marrying

78

someone we became fascinated with before learning their character, desires, and especially, what is in their hearts.

"Find love with all your heart. And once found, love will find you. It will break away the unbreakable and make anew."

Anthony Liccione

People who are obsessed with wanting a spouse may never find one. It is better to just relax and wait. God will bring a mate to you. A wonderful place to find a mate is at a church. Stay after church. Many churches have a coffee room which is a beautiful place for a Christian to find a Christian.

When a person lives alone and feels lonely, just relax, and know you are not alone. God is with you.

"I will never forsake you. I'll never leave you."

Hebrews 13:6

I AM NOT HAPPY

Why do so many people think other people are making them unhappy? As I explained in my first book in detail, we are solely responsible for creating our own happiness. The reality of the situation is that on the physical plane of our life, we are born alone and will be lowered into our graves on our lonesome.

Nobody will present the world's gifts to you with a silver spoon; only through challenging work, keeping our faith in our Lord, and having steeled determination can we experience happiness.

79

It is not our parent's or spouses' responsibility to always help us. We are not usually the ones that manage it to our friends, boss, or anyone else. We must think and act in a way that will make us happy. If we make the wrong decisions that make us unhappy, we alone are responsible for transforming the patterns of our thought processes and acting accordingly.

We should start by learning to be content with what we have.

"But godliness with contentment is great gain. For we brought nothing into the world, and we can take nothing out of it. But if we have food and clothing, we will be content with that."

1 Timothy 6:6-12

If we expect more than that, then it is our responsibility to produce a plan to get more.

This takes research and a lot of challenges that unhappy people need to leap over to reach a state where they are fulfilled. It is easier to wallow in their unhappiness and complain. Also, we must build humility, a modest or realistic view of one's importance.

We may be unhappy because we lack humility and humbleness as well. We feel alone, and that makes us unhappy. If that is the case, we lack God in our hearts. When we keep God in our lives, we are never alone every day; thus, we have faith in something other than ourselves. When we sleep, God never slumbers, nor does He rest. His Spirit lives within Christians who accept Jesus as Lord and Savior. If we bury it, we must dig it back out, or we will continue to feel alone.

"Instead of pursuing happiness, pursue God and happiness will find you deep in your soul."

Leila Grandemange

80

Another reason many are unhappy is that they turn to drugs or alcohol to find happiness. I was guilty of this once in my life, so I am not being critical here. None of us grew up being angels, and the Devil tempts us to use drugs and alcohol as a form of escapism. He makes them seem like innocent fun where the "giggles" make us laugh hysterically so hard that we will never stop.

In time, the fun reduces to just falling asleep. The result turns to sadness, depression, failure, and a drop in our level of consciousness. And when we wish for more, this dependency becomes an addiction where we harm our bodies and others around us.

This drop in consciousness causes an equal drop in our health, happiness, and our success.

"Happiness already exists in your life. All you need to do is tune into it. And you can start doing that right now."

Anthon St. Maarten

I AM OVERWHELMED

We all become overwhelmed at various times. If we plan to change our life, we need to stop this. A huge problem or too many problems keep punching at us, and we do not know what to do first. Making it worse, we become exhausted, and we do not have the energy to get life back to normal. In doing so, we accumulate a huge amount of stress that drops us close to the lowest level of our consciousness. We become physically and mentally overpowered by this elevated level of stress.

81

Exhausted, we lose self-control and become slow, confused, forgetful, and upset. We find it hard to sleep and cannot think logically and rationally anymore. Our minds race with monkey jump thinking of the many problems we are trying to juggle. Becoming emotionally overwhelmed, we are unable to face daily life duties. We just have too much to oversee, and we cannot do it anymore.

We must get out of the habit of dropping things, yelling at red lights, and swearing at rude drivers. This requires us to slow down, take a break, and take deep breaths until we feel calmer and in control.

This, of course, will affect our relationships with others. Being in such a traumatic state of mind, we feel we are letting our wives, children, bosses, and everyone down. Unless we do something to release our levels of stress and rise in both our level of consciousness and in our inner power, we will feel powerless. We need to stop worrying and get going with solutions. It starts with taking the first step.

"We Generate Fears While We Sit. We Overcome Them by Action."

Dr. Henry Link

Those of you who read my first book understand that when we are low in consciousness, we are exceptionally low in our power to do things. The two triangles, depicting our level of consciousness against our level of inner power, are in the introduction of this back. In case you did not read it, stop here, and

82

go back to read it as there is particularly essential information that will be of help to you.

We shut down and sometimes put our head in our hands while we suffer and beg God for help.

"Our hope for you is steadfast because we know that you are partakers of the suffering, so also you will be of the consolation,"

2 Corinthians 1:7

The problem can only improve if we take strong positive actions to eliminate negative thoughts. Then, when we feel better, we must make a list of everything that is bothering us. When we are overwhelmed, the list is too long to complete in one day. We must prioritize the list, starting with the most important things on our list, usually our family. Make a list for today that is comfortable to complete, with extra driving time built in and time for yourself, like stopping for a coffee or lunch.

Chapter 6

ADDICTIONS

FAMILY ADDICTION PROBLEM

There are all kinds of addicts in addition to drugs and alcohol. As mentioned above, such substances may seem innocent initially, but if they become a part of your daily habits, they will lead to devastation. But other than substances, other forms of temptation exist. We ignore that due to their insignificant nature.

People become addicted to all day and evening television, glued to cell phones and whatever consumes their hearts.

Whenever they hear a cell notification signal, they immediately pick up the phone and start doing other things. That is just what the creators of this want, as they make millions of dollars from those addicted to phones. They cannot even go to the gym without that cell and sit on machines, tying them up while others wait, checking their phones. When anything other than the truth of God consumes the bulk of our day, we are addicted.

Many have an addiction to television and watch CNN or soap operas all day long. Then after supper, they watch their favorite shows or movies for five or six hours. This can be reduced by reducing the time spent talking, walking, reading, writing, playing music, or whatever.

84

Totally avoid devil-influenced movies on television or your cell or computer. It is best to avoid many types of shows, such as violence, horror movies, and pornography. If we watch TV, we must be selective about what we watch. It is good to be in the Word every day to avoid creating your own troubled times.

Watch Christian speakers on YouTube, such as Andrew Wommack, and listen to words that inspire you and guide you to salvation whilst making sure that you live a fulfilled life on this Earth. Practical but spiritual, and their words will aid you in moments of loneliness and weakness.

A narcotics addict is living in a real-life hell, in torture, when needing a fix. In many cases, they begin to steal from those who love them. Addiction takes away all moral character when an addict needs a fix. I would like every addict to understand that there does not exist anywhere in the world any illegal narcotic that can make life worthwhile and meaningful.

In most cases, when we become addicted, we affect those we live with and take away their joy, bringing them sheer grief, anger, and disappointment, and we can list many other bad feelings. But the addict does not care. Addiction has taken over their lives, and they become consumed with the hell they are living in.

I must agree that, in many cases, others can cause one to become an addict. We have a friend who talks us into trying drugs or drinking numerous shots to get drunk. But it is our choice, and there is only one choice: to get rid of anyone who is causing you this damage, go for help, and cast the addiction out of our total being with the help of God, consuming his word all day long.

"What would Jesus do?" We can use that when trying to decide if we should do something or not. You argue that as normal humans, no one can be Jesus and thus worthy enough to follow his examples, but we can try and better ourselves.

85

There is always some space for improvement; therefore, try using the "Golden Rule" or say only what we want others to do or say to us.

No, it is never fun to live in sin.

Many addicts seize sinful opportunities to provide for their addictions. Thus, some people often become prostitutes working for a pimp who feeds them drugs. The pimps often beat up their girls when they do not bring home enough money. I feel sorry for these girls who were captured by the wickedness and snarls of the devil. They are living a life of hell, but they can take steps to get out.

"Remember, just because you hit bottom doesn't mean you have to stay there."

Robert Downey

You will stay as an addict until you break yourself away from your addictions. There is no shame in seeking help, like joining a bible-based Christian church and seeking help from the members who will also lead us to others we may need. Also, seek therapy along with bible-based gatherings. The church will help you accept Jesus as our Lord and savior to be rebirthed from your sins. In doing so, our spirit becomes perfect and is powerful as Jesus.

"Truly, I tell you, if you have faith as small as a mustard seed, you can say to this mountain, 'Move from here to there,' and it will move. Nothing will be impossible for you."

Matthew 17:20-21

This is the start of beating the addiction with the help of Christian fellowship.

86

Someone there can also help prostitutes in the prisons of pimps get free from them. What are the things we give up to battle addictions?

Hatred, sadness, lack of self-control, depression, pain, and anger? Upon giving up a life of hell, we beat our demons along with the devil's temptations.

Mind you, this is not an easy feat. Finding salvation requires patience and determination. There is no easy alternative for battling addictions and sickness.

ADDICTION TO PORNOGRAPHY

"Let us behave decently, as in the daytime, not in carousing and drunkenness, not in sensual immorality and debauchery, not in dissension and jealousy. Rather, clothe yourselves with the Lord Jesus Christ, and do not think about how to gratify the desires of the flesh."

Romans 13:13-14

We all were blessed with a conscience. When we get addicted to pornography, our conscious will try its best to make us stop.

The devil wants to get people addicted to porn. He knows we have a conscious and human nature. Quite simply, a human always has a need to procreate, it may be a deep-rooted desire, but if triggered, it can take hold of our consciousness akin to a wave crashing against a shore.

If our consciousness is not tempered enough, he starts with a minor temptation, for example, sneaking a magazine filled with risqué pictures in a mart when no one was looking. Then he will

87

push one to a sexy R-rated movie. *R-rating* is not so bad, and the devil will lie.

But each step is not satisfying. So, he prompts one to watch an X-rated movie. Again, there is no real satisfaction in porn, so it just worsens.

With the advent of the Internet, most men heard about free sex movies, and curiosity killed the cat. They slowly were tempted, as in the above, to get worse and worse until addictions set in, and porn addicts spend hours each day trying to find something they never will find, and they continue to get bored.

"Whatever sows to please their flesh, from the flesh will reap destruction; whoever sows to please the Spirit, from the Spirit will reap eternal life."

Galatians 6:8

Many found more satisfaction in the videos than in their own wives. Eventually, the women get suspicious, catch them at it, and the trouble begins, often ending in divorce.

Parents need to monitor what their teenage children watch to prevent them from not only porno addiction but the many other forms of devil-supported, God hates evil websites, devil workshops, dark music, gruesome pictures, pornography, or any form of sinful conduct.

It corrupts your children's demeanor and ruins the chance of finding a happy life on Earth or in the afterlife.

"Flee from sexual immorality."

1 Corinthians 6:18

If you know anyone entering websites that are wrong for anyone to be watching, push them into getting help, like

Alcoholics Anonymous. Churches will offer support as well. If you are into any of this, do not be embarrassed. Acknowledging your faults is the first step to finding salvation; no one will judge someone looking for help in the right places.

Anyone with this addiction must give it up "cold turkey" and move on to alternatives to better spend free time.

"Consuming pornography does not lead to more sex; it leads to more porn. Much like eating at McDonald's every day will accustom you to food that, although enjoyable, is essentially not food, pornography conditions the consumer to being satisfied with an impression of extreme sex rather than the real."

Virginie Despentes

ALCOHOLISM

Alcohol may seem harmless at first. You have a glass with your friends at a party. You clink another on the dinner table with your family, and you have another in celebration of an event.

Pleasantries will eventually turn into habits; therefore, alcohol will bring chaos to the drinker and others who love them. It is a chronic disease that becomes uncontrollable to the alcoholic. It starts with one who drinks every day.

A husband who must stop in a bar every night after work with his friends will drink there. Midnight tolls, and he brings a case of beer home. This cycle continues once or twice, and drinking becomes a daily habit rather than a ceremonial gesture. The more they drink, the more they have urges to drink. No harm, right? Just

89

beer? Wrong. You become an alcoholic by drinking a lot of beer daily. Then, beer is not quick enough when the hands start shaking. Shots of hard liquor work quicker. Then they began to lose appetite and weight.

Smokers will sit in their chairs or on a couch, drinking, and smoking until they pass out. Not only does this lifestyle affect their health but their environment as well. Passive smoking places compromise the health of the people around them. Numerous fires start due to smokers falling asleep with a lit cigarette in their hands. If they try to stop, they have withdrawal symptoms. Like a virus that seeps the life force from its host, alcoholism is a demon that hollows its host from the inside.

They need treatment, counseling, behavioral therapy, and medications that reduce the desire to drink. They may need medical detoxification to stop drinking safely. Some join alcoholics anonymous, as they need to be in a support group to avoid relapses. They need a lifestyle change, especially giving up drinking with friends and frequenting bars. Once they stop, they cannot cheat as it will have the same result as a drug addict deciding to get just one fix.

Just becoming aware of one's lifestyle and company can bring about an impactful change. Alcohol abuse is a major problem among college students who participate in binge drinking. At first, we enjoyed it because it is fun, and everyone is doing it! Drinking parties are commonplace in colleges, with consequences that include alcohol toxicity and, in some cases, death. It causes a breakdown of the immune system, which we know is the cause of most illnesses. It also causes reckless driving and accidents, frequently injuring or killing others and, sometimes, themselves.

"One cannot live a life of full-time 'partying' and sustain the prohibitive cost of supporting a family or self."

Matt Jordan

Not just students but people of all ages who drink too much and then get behind the wheel to drive home are making a huge mistake. Driving under the influence is dangerous, all of us who have tried that in our younger days know that our judgment is impaired. But we brush the danger off in favor of the thrill, and we risk not only our own lives but also the lives of others.

Alcohol poisoning is a danger related to drinking due to the ethanol contained in alcohol. Ethanol could damage the central nervous system. Brain function slows down, causing a lack of coordination, blurred vision, and slurred speech. During extreme binge drinking, your body cannot dissolve ethanol safely. Binge drinking over time can lead to poor memory, brain cell and memory loss, violent behavior, depression, and coma.

For many, it has led to death.

"Always do sober what you said you'd do when you were drunk. That will teach you to keep your mouth shut!"

Ernest Hemingway

91

Chapter 7

RELATIONSHIPS

I LIKE PEOPLE, BUT...

"I like people, but they all really upset me."

Guess what? Most of us, at times, upset others as well. I call it the polar two sides of personality. Most good characteristics that we possess have an opposite negative side. I will use myself as an example. When I built several successful businesses in my younger years, I was known to be an aggressive, tough, soldering-ahead type of person who set my goals and aggressively fought hard until I had them.

What is the opposite of this aggressive characteristic? It is stubbornness. The kind of stubbornness that does not let anything get in the way of reaching my goals. What are some of the major obstacles in one's life? Distractions such as people and other activities do not allow for growth. The biggest obstacles I have experienced are people who cannot fathom the progress of others. To veil their insecurities, people often cause problems for others as they are jealous of achievers.

As I began getting older and understood this strange concept of jealousy and the polar sides of personality, I began to change, or at least control it. We are born with good and bad characteristics

92

that we have. Unfortunately, we tend to lean towards the bad because the world often conditions us in that light. Therefore, as Lincoln said:

"If we look for the bad in people, we will surely find it."

Abraham Lincoln.

It took me years to understand this, long after I heard it in school. I went to a tough manager's class once. After a couple of weeks of all of us talking and we got to know each other quite well, the instructor made us each make good and bad points about each of the others in the class. No one had to sign their names.

Then the teacher put them all together and read them to us one by one. No one was happy with the negative things that were said. I decided I wanted to know what others truly thought about me, so I took the comments to heart and began controlling the negatives using self-control. It is not easy to listen to someone tell us the things we are doing that annoy them.

But to fully develop into the person God created us to be, we must ask others to honestly tell us how we can improve. Then we must take it to heart and try hard not to manifest the bad side of our character.

Try it with your family and those you spend a lot of time with. Without getting angry, steal your consciousness and show them that you control your temperament. Before you end up mistakenly hating people, consider what Jesus had to say.

"If the world hates you, know that it had hated me before it hated you."

John 15:18

93

PEOPLE HATE ME

"Often the rich are hated, and worse yet, the poor are despised."

Matt Jordan

Some people will hate us because of our race, color, creed, political beliefs, or because we are poor people beneath them. Hate is one of the core elements in humanity's makeup. Since time's beginning, hate has been the forerunner in creating numerous wars.

Where should we draw the line? You should never seek the friendship of those who are bigots and those who spread this corrosive disease. These are people who do not make good friends. Do not be concerned whether they like you or not.

If people hate you for other reasons, you need to ask yourself whether you like them. People will instinctively not like you if they feel you do not like them. People will instinctively not like us if we consciously or subconsciously dislike them. But, if people hate us because of our conduct, we need to ask them why and do some self-analysis.

We may have to change our behavior in front of people. It could be doing something that turns people off.

How do people decide whether they like us? For most people, it has nothing to do with race, color, creed, fat, skinny, money, tall or short. It has more to do with our personality and conduct as we interact with the world and the people around us.

Do we act depressed all the time? Are we negative on all subjects? Are we comfortable to be with? Are we too bossy when making decisions on what we will do with friends? Are we on time to meet our friends? Do we take time to compliment others? Are we judgmental and critical of others too often? Or do we do or say things that make others dislike us?

If not, and they are just treating you badly, they will face the wrath of God.

"I tell you the truth, when you did it to one of the least of these my brothers and sisters, you were doing it to me!"

Matthew 25:40

We can only gain the confidence of others when we fully develop confidence within ourselves. Remember, it is our conduct that makes others hate or like us. They go by the things we say and do.

Take time to ask your friends how they feel about your personality. View it as constructive criticism, but ask someone you can trust. Also, do not be shy to let other people know how you feel about them, including compliments and kind pleasantries.

"I like you a lot." It is just five words.

I would like your opinion on something. What can I do or say to make you like me more? Then listen without getting defensive, or they may stop before they are done speaking. Do you want to make people love you? Love them first and be a good friend to them. Treat others as you want to be treated by others. Winning a friendship is light years more valuable than winning games or money.

Some who hate you are not worth your time.

"The wicked envy and hate; it is their way of admiring."

Victor Hugo

If good people do not like you, you need to find out why and change your conduct and impression. Here is one sure way you can

95

make others like you. Try to act like Jesus. In every action, think, "What would Jesus do or say?" Study His conduct and his relationship with people. Register how He cared for everyone without prejudice.

Watch movies on Jesus to listen to how he talked with people and how he treated people. If you talk and act like Jesus, I guarantee that people will love you. But remember to be easy on yourself and never change yourself completely for people because you cannot please everyone.

"Put on tender mercies with compassion, kindness, humility, gentleness, and patience."

Colossians 3:12

HATING POLITICIANS

We must stay in control when others upset us, especially politicians. Many wonder how so many politicians became multimillionaires on their salaries. Many have been dishonest and want the jobs for personal gain rather than to help the public.

Remember, newscasters usually report sad news, which sells more than good news. As I mentioned, we must limit our time on the news to avoid getting depressed. We need to control outside influences and not be affected by them. We do not want to develop hopelessness. We can all help by voting for new politicians who are honest and respect history. If we hate politicians, then we need to help get them out of office.

We must stay strong. We cannot change the world, but we can get rid of dishonest politicians who have been in power far too long. We need to control our health, happiness, and success and not let politicians cause us anxiety or affect how we think when their platforms are not supporting our constitution, laws, and freedom.

Politicians can cause negative thinking. Remember, you are their boss. You can help fire them if you take the time to vote in every election. Too many good people think my vote will not be effective. Unfortunately, in many elections, the best candidate did not win because too many people thought their vote would not count. Every vote does count.

"Bad politicians are sent to Washington by good people who do not vote."

William E. Simon

I personally think we must vote in term limits as too many politicians with many years of experience end up becoming millionaires despite not having that much salary. Too many of them get too embedded with people they get to know around the world.

You hate politicians. Not all people are bad. Vote for politicians after checking them out. Consider it a job interview. We cannot vote for one because of their looks or gift of gab.

97

CAN NOT FORGIVE OTHERS

"Forgiveness is a gift you give yourself."

Tony Robbins

When one does an injustice with the intent to harm us, we must forgive them, not for their sake, but for our sake. If we do not, we cannot free ourselves from the invisible yoke we have attached to them. If not, we remain hooked on them all the rest of our life, causing us to be angry and bitter.

We cannot find happiness when we feel this way. It can even make us sick.

Understand that forgiving someone who offended us does not mean we have to forget. Some wrongs are so bad that they are impossible to forget. But we must let it go, or it will affect us for the rest of our lives.

"Bless them which persecute you; bless, and curse not."

Romans 12:14

Also, we do not have to forgive them in person. We can forgive them alone as part of our prayers. We do not have to remain their friend or go out for coffee or dinner with them.

In fact, we do not have to ever deal with them again unless they live in our circle, family, job, or whatever. We just need to be courteous, say a quick hello, and keep walking.

It is not difficult to forgive someone if we understand that God has promised to avenge all bad deeds. Vengeance is God's, not ours. We must trust in Him to not let the offender off the hook. They will be punished.

"If your enemy is hungry, feed him;
If he is thirsty, give him something to drink.
In doing this, you will heap burning coals on his head."

Romans 12:20

DIVORCE

When someone does not think their spouse is their best friend, their marriage is in trouble. When we meet and marry a spouse that we know we are "in love" with, we start out being each other's best friend. We are just miserable when we are apart and cannot wait until we are back together.

We frequently call or text each other. Then we get married and often stop being best friends.

This "best friend" attitude and commitment must continue to keep the marriage healthy. We must put each other first. It is a mistake when that best friend changes and the spouse fall back to putting old friends first.

While an amount of time with old friends is even an innovative idea for both the husband and the wife, like anything else, it must be done in reasonable moderation.

One reasonable course of action would be to take one night a week for each to go out with a friend, preferably of the opposite-sex. Yes, the devil will pick away at opposite-sex friendships for some people who give in to the temptation to cheat.

Marriage is difficult as it is. It certainly helps to put your spouse first, and beyond house duties and sleep, you go out and do things as "best friends."

99

A second problem happens when a marriage is consummated with the couple just being infatuated for at least a year, which feels just like being "in love." Unfortunately, infatuations fade like a pot of steaming water cooling off. Infatuated couples will usually end up in divorce. However, some couples who marry, being just infatuated, have their relationship grow into "love." Unfortunately, we cannot control the heart and therefore cannot control whether we want to, or do not want to be, "in love." We cannot turn it on or off.

In addition to the possibility that two people married, only being infatuated, there is another cause of divorce. Back in the day when *Sex, Drugs, and Rock and Roll* were the things, couples had a lot of fun together and misinterpreted this as being "in love." Many of them married; however, many did not marry "in love." They married *in lust*, and there is a stark difference.

The devil has us thinking that sex, drugs, and rock and roll are innocent at first, but all addictions appear like this. He does this for any addiction to lure us in. However, when we marry for the wrong reasons, and sex is no longer enough to be the yoke that keeps the marriage bonded, the marriage is doomed from the beginning.

Again, there are exceptions, as couples in this category also can fall "in love" at some point after marriage.

No matter how hard we try to save the marriage, it is exceedingly difficult if we are no longer "in love," it is a steep uphill and an impossible battle.

You can seek counseling, church help, or whatever, but you simply cannot save a marriage that did not have love as a base. The foundation was mud, not stone.

My wife is my best friend. We go for walks, dinner, travel, do all sorts of things together, and enjoy the fun we have together. We do not tire of this, and each year gets better. Like any couple living together, we sometimes have differences and must learn to compromise or agree to disagree.

However, when two or more people live together, there will be differences and arguments. Ultimately, each must learn to compromise, and no one should always get their way. Without compromise and each spouse being fair, the marriage starts crumbling.

This is painful to everyone in the family.

"In all friendship hearts grow and entwine themselves together, so that the two hearts seem to make only one heart with only a common thought. That is why separation is so painful; it is not so much two hearts separating, but one being torn asunder."

Bishop Fulton J. Sheen

Divorce is more difficult if we have children, as the children will always want us to get back together if we separate. Not to mention the psychological impact on their developing psyches. Often, we are so involved in our matters that we do not see the eyes of our children, experiencing the breaking of their family that they thought was meant to last forever.

Therefore, many live in failed marriages because they stay together because they think it is best for their children. In these difficult days of unreasonable prices, we cannot afford to split and pay for two separate households.

A failed marriage is hard to get through. It can be as bad as the death of a loved one. Even if we do not fight in front of the children, the atmosphere gets so cold one can cut it with a knife. We cannot fool children.

They will suffer when their parents fight or give each other the cold shoulder. Often, a separation consists of one-party having custody and the other having visitation rights to spend quality time with the children.

This is much better mentally for the children than living together like roommates. The children sense something is wrong, not seeing hugs and kisses and noticing the cold tone.

Again, I speak on all of this from personal experience, so I understand.

Regardless of the situations above, love is the key to avoiding divorce. Without love, it just does not work, and you just will annoy each other. We must give love to get love back. Marriage and love take consistent, challenging work every day.

"Love is patient, love is kind. It does not envy, it does not boast, it is not proud."

1 Corinthians 13:4

SPOUSE CHEATED

We marry for better or for worse and till death do us part. Marriage is a bond that seals the lives of two strangers into one. We do not think too deeply into the mysticism of the bond, for we are lost in the blinding glamor.

Marriage requires us to be patient, loving and, most importantly, loyal to our spouse. Very few types of mental anguish are worse than finding out your spouse cheated. While it is usually the husband who cheats, no doubt some wives cheat as well.

Either way, it is wrong. Cheating breaks not only the relationship but the persons involved.

Many young husbands think they love their wives, but they cheat "just for fun." I admit I made this mistake, and it cost me my marriage. While we all make mistakes, at some point, we must change our ways and do what is right.

"It does not mean anything," they tell their wives. However, if a spouse finds out about the cheating, man, or woman, it is tragic, demeaning, and extremely upsetting. To retrieve any level of trust again is next to impossible, and to forgive is exceedingly difficult. As I have written before, it will be impossible to ever forget the act of cheating.

Certainly, a wife will cry a river of tears, feeling helpless, depressed, and deeply hurt. Many will lose their self-esteem, thinking they are simply not good enough. The husband may try to say, "I had too many drinks. I promise it will never happen again."

Before the couple just ends it and files for a divorce, they must first decide this: were we ever in love, or was it just an infatuation that burned out over time?

If the couple both felt that they were truly in love, they should go to marriage counseling, talk it all out, and try to save the marriage. Their church may have someone qualified to help, but they should have a third party monitor a plan of action to save the marriage with vows never to cheat again.

If both parties are truly in love, it is worth forgiving and giving the cheating spouse one chance to stop the cheating. But the cheating spouse must remain loyal to the spouse who was violated.

We need to sit down and talk about what went wrong and whether we were ever truly "in love" or was the basis just infatuation. Couples should not marry until they are together for at least a year to understand whether they are in love or simply infatuated.

103

"In a marriage, in any long-term relationship, do not bother with lying. There's no time for that. If you have any sort of secret life, it will come back to haunt you."

Andy Garcia

I WILL NEVER MARRY AGAIN

Many people who came out of a troubled marriage will say, "I will never get married again."

Those who also face hardships and heartbreaks from the opposite gender will claim that they will never marry to avoid their past from repeating. That is sad because no one should feel this way.

Marriage is a harmonious alliance between two people. People need to realize that nobody can find their pre-made happily ever-after. Everyone is different and has flaws, and it is what makes us human. If we are tolerant, patient, and communicative with each other, we have a best friend to love and grow old together with for the rest of our life.

Just because someone had one or more unhappy marriages does not mean that you cannot fall in love and enjoy the many benefits of marriage. You just must be sure each party is fully "in love" with the other.

Most marriages fail because they should never have happened in the first place. Many marry too soon after meeting someone. I do believe in "love at first sight," but that is normally not the case.

Usually, it takes at least a year to know that both parties are more than infatuated but are truly "in love."

Your spouse cheated on you, and you think everyone will cheat. The truth is, in a happy marriage, when your partner is your best friend and your number one priority, the marriage gets better each year, and there is no need to cheat. It would help if you took the time to learn about the character of the spouse who cheated. Is the person a God-fearing, loving Christian? Without God in a marriage, your chances of success are limited.

The courting period is not the way to select a spouse, especially since each party is acting their best, using the sweetest of words, and not being themselves. Will such a partner be a good parent? Does the partner want to be a parent? Is the partner an egotist, only into him or herself, vain and shallow? You must discuss and see if you agree on all subjects, like children, moving distances, housing, vacations, and time with other friends. You really must know everything about each other.

So, in conclusion, never think you will ever marry again. Just take the time to do it right next time, but never ever decide never to get married again. The joy between two married individuals who are in love and best friends can never be beaten by living alone.

Chapter 8

DAILY PROBLEMS

I HATE MY JOB

Eighty percent of Americans hate their job.

The reason is simple: It is because they are not doing the field of work God created them to do. If you do what you were born to do, you will not work a single day of your life because you will have fun doing it.

"Let us run with perseverance the race marked out for us, fixing our eyes on Jesus, the pioneer and perfecter of faith.'

Hebrews 12:1-2

So, if we hate our job, we must first decide whether we are doing the field of work marked out for us by our creator. If we are, we will enjoy our work for the rest of our lives. If we are not enjoying our job, we are not doing the right kind of work. We picked any job available, or our parents pushed us into it. No matter what the reason, if we do not choose a field of work that we love, we are not working in the right job, and we will hate it.

We need to decide the "who, what, where, when, why, and how." I wish to change the order as follows. What, why, where,

106

how, who, and when. That is the order that makes more sense as each decision leads to the following decision.

If we are not sure of what we would like to do, pray on it. God has given you a mission, and He will answer your prayer.

"Father, let Thy will, and not my will be done."

Luke 22:42.

Listen to your inner self. Trust your instincts. Analyze why it is that we want to do this. Is it something we really want to do, or are we making that decision because someone told us that there is a need for that line of work? For example, we may be advised to become a programmer because there is a huge need for programmers, and they make good money. However, if you love writing poems or literature, you will hate being a programmer.

Then we should decide where we want to do it. To have the best chance for success, we should study the demographics of the work we want to do. Where is there a need, and where is the market? What is the income and education level in that market? If it is in the field of real estate, where is the best place to conduct our goal? Find a growing area, and there will be many opportunities. If we try real estate in a dead area many are moving out of, we have little chance of success.

You will hear many success teachers say that there are three important decisions to make to achieve success. They are location, location, and location. We need to plan exactly how we are going to make this goal happen. We will list all the tasks necessary we must do to bring the goal to fruition.

Then we need to decide who will do this. For example, if we are planning a business, who are the types of people that suit our goals best? Is there a special place to find them? For example, if we want to build a successful technology business, there are many great tech companies in Southern California.

Finally, we must decide when to do this. We need to list the tasks necessary to get there and put a completion date next to each task. All goals should be "measurable" so that we can monitor our success. If we are shooting for the moon and we find ourselves going off course, we need to make the correction immediately.

I think that too many people fear starting work to pursue their dreams. Some of them procrastinate because of their fear of failure. That is a serious mistake. Our desire to succeed should be light years more important to us than our fear of failure. Once we complete all these tasks, we need to get the education and experience necessary to succeed.

"Things may come to those who wait, but only the things left by those who hustle."

Abraham Lincoln

MY LIFE IS WORTHLESS

No life is worthless. God created each one of us to have a purpose. If our life is worthwhile to God, surely it is worthwhile for us to live. No life is worthless. If we think that we need to seek help to determine what we are doing wrong. We already discussed that if we are unhappy, we may be in the wrong job, as I discussed previously.

Now we need to go deeper and clear up any issues negatively reflecting self-esteem. This is necessary if we are going to work on a plan to identify and carry our purpose in life. Often those who have not achieved anything worthwhile pretend to be someone they are not. This is a mistake.

"The greatest way to live with honor in this world is to be what we pretend to be."

Socrates

It is better to be the person that we want to be and do whatever it is that we must do to make our life worthwhile. We already discussed why so many hate their job and how to determine what we are born to do and when we do that, we will never work another day of our life. We will be doing what we were born to do, and we will enjoy the work very much.

Once we know what that work is, we must write down some goals to get educated and qualified to do so. We, at that point, will already stop feeling worthless as we will enjoy the entire process of getting into an enjoyable job or business. We will feel self-esteem, and we will rejoice.

"Rejoice always, pray continually, give thanks in all circumstances, for this is God's will for you in Christ Jesus."

1 Thessalonian 5:16-18

If we feel our life has not been worthwhile, regardless of age, we need to get going. The hardest step is the first step. Once you take that, you will keep moving. Do you remember this point in science?

"Bodies in motion tend to stay in motion; bodies at rest tend to stay at rest."

If we think our life is not worthwhile, we need to get busy. We must determine the field of work that we would love to do, we need to get a book on careers within that line of work. If we are in school, we should see a career guidance counselor. Then we must

109

find out exactly what the requirements are to do that work and get the education and experience. If it is the field of music, there are many kinds of jobs within that field, like teaching, writing, arranging, and performing. If it is the field of medicine, we can become a doctor, nurse, or assistant.

When we believe that we have the power to achieve any goal, we develop faith in the successful results that we believe are forthcoming.

"Jesus said to him, 'Everything is possible to the one who believes.'"

Mark 9:23

Once you start this path to happiness and self-esteem, do not just talk about it. Do it.

"Well done is better than well said."

Benjamin Franklin

BAD PEOPLE ARE AFTER ME

Stay away from bad people like they are the plague, or they surely will bring you into tough times. Whether they are pimps, drug dealers, mobsters, bookies, women beaters, loan sharks, or whatever, they will be after you one day when you try to break away from them.

Do not let them get to know you in the first place. If you do not talk to them and ignore any advances from them by "keep walking," in most cases, they will not bother you. But let us say, "Too late, Matt. I already made the mistake. I have someone after me that I should never have gotten involved with. What should I do?"

Start by nicely saying, "I have serious problems in my life. I appreciate all you did, but I cannot see you anymore."

So that may or may not work, but it is a necessary step you must take before you take the next step. If they do not accept that and come to hit you, or threaten you, try to always have a recorder set so you can record the conversation by turning the recorder on your cell phone in your pocket before you see them. After the talk, walk away. Go to the police to make a report and then to the court for an "order of protection." If they violate it, call the police, and they will go to jail.

This is scary. But get help from friends, relatives, a church, or a support group, so you do not have to go through it alone. If you are living alone and you have someone you can go live with until the problem smooths over, go as they will be witnesses when you call the police again. Get tough. Stand up for yourselves and get whoever is after you out of your life. But do not try to do it without support. Going to the police is best.

TONGUE CONTROL

"Whoever of you loves life and desires to see many good days, keep your tongue from evil."

Psalm 34:12-13

The tongue has a strength factor somewhere between 40-80 kilopascals, averaging about sixty-three. That is not extraordinarily strong. However, its damage can be immeasurable. We cannot take back the things that we say. They are indelible in the minds of those we hurt forever. We should not harshly criticize others to the point of tearing them down and destroying their self-esteem. Even if we apologize, they may forgive us, but they will never forget our harsh words. It could reflect our relationship with the person violated for the rest of the violated person's life.

"Even so the tongue is a little member and boasts great things; see how a great forest is set on fire by a small spark."

James 3:5

Our tongue was meant to speak words with the glory of God. He wanted us to bless others, not abuse them, bringing sorrow and even tears. Our speech reflects our character. We should not be grumbling, blaspheming, boasting, discriminating, or chastising others.

"...and thus, the tongue can be used for both good and evil."

James 3:9

Our tongue has the power to make people do things. We can direct them on a rightful or wrongful course. We can help direct others out of sin and any path leading to destruction. We should not use our tongues to curse, lie, or crush the spirits of those we

112

are speaking to. Think before you say. Speak slowly so you can do so. Focus on listening before you speak to think first about what you are going to say.

"Bad words create never-ending, bad feelings."

Matt Jordan

Like deadly poison, our words can corrupt others' lives into a living hell. Without control, our words can corrupt a person and affect them for life. Many have even committed suicide due to constant chastising and the loss of their entire self-respect. When we are angry, we must think before we talk. If we are angry at someone, before we speak, we should take a deep breath, relax, calm down, and find a tactful way of suggesting rather than using a scathing tongue.

"He who restrains his lips is wise."

Proverbs 10:19

We must understand that when we are hurting others, we also hurt God. Here is a suggestion. When someone verbally attacks us, rather than scream back and get into a fight that leads to both parties being hurt and nobody winning, shock them but saying something nice.

"A soft word turns away wrath, but a harsh word stirs up anger."

Proverbs 15:1

We need to take control of our tongue and not let it sound off, aimlessly, especially when unleashing a tirade of negative criticism. If not, it will always lead to a problem for us.

Lack of control over the tongue gets many of us in trouble or causes grave danger to those we are offending. We must get rid of all bitterness and anger as they cause us to "mouth off," at others,

113

unnecessarily. We must instead be compassionate to others and forgive them when they offend us. If we want to be forgiven, then the Lord requires us to forgive.

"On the one hand, the tongue is very religious, but on the other, it can be most profane."

Peter Davids

DIVISIVENESS

Divisiveness is caused by complete disagreement and, in many cases, hostility between people. Unfortunately, the divisiveness in the United States at the time of this writing is extremely hostile. The questions are, why is there so much dissension and discord between political parties? Should both parties not want whatever is best for all people?

We, the people trying to get the people to unite and work together for the betterment of the country, are frustrated because people get angry when we discuss this. Are people so brainwashed by fake news that they do not want to objectively discuss the right and wrong between political differences?

I try to push those who disagree to place their platforms up against scripture. Are we supporting platforms that are not within the rules of God? Are we promoting sin? Why? Are outside anti-forces trying to destroy the country as a world power? I will not take sides in this book, but ask people of both parties to think on each disagreement; what would Jesus do? We all know that both parties have done some terrible things.

114

Also, there is divisiveness within families and married couples for many of the same reasons. Many of us are finding it best not to discuss politics with anyone from the opposite party to avoid arguments. I have never seen our country so divided as it is now. Disagreements, political differences, hostility between friends and relatives, group arguments, on and on.

This can cause depression, anger, hatred, and other negative feelings that can push us into tough times, making everything much worse. So, what do we do about it? We must form two groups that disagree with us. The first group is friends, and the second group is close relatives. Those who are just friends or acquaintances should know not to talk about politics. If any friends do not honor that, then we may want to consider releasing them as friends. However, that is not so easy with relatives.

What I do with my relatives is agreeing to disagree. That must be followed by an agreement that neither side will ever bring the subject, especially when the differences are in either religion or in politics. No couple should push their marriage into divorce because of political disagreements. Just do not talk about it or comment about it. Also, avoid the news, or do not watch it together.

Chapter 9

EXTERNAL ISSUES

NEWS UPSETS ME

I usually limit my time watching the news to about 10 minutes each morning. I simply want to hear if anything bad is going on about which I should know. I do not enjoy news stations that sit around discussing upsetting news all day. Many have news on their televisions all day long. This affects how we feel. It makes us worry unnecessarily. It makes many feel depressed. Some do not watch the news at all, and there is a good case for that.

Whatever you let feed your mind will affect your level of consciousness. Constant unwelcome news will take you to a much lower level. We all now know that this also takes you down in health, happiness, and success. World news has changed.

We used to watch the news to find out what was happening locally and globally. But at some point, starting around the year 2000, the news changed. Cable news features people sitting around on set, or on inserted cameras, talking all day about their "opinions" rather than reporting actual news. Evil people began making billions of dollars, scaring people with manufactured news. When people are selling stocks, they are buying, and when

Joe Taxi is buying, they are selling. Markets are manipulated by the super-rich at times.

Inflation kept rising at the writing of this book in 2022. As inflation exploded, prices began skyrocketing for housing, rents, food, heating oil, supplies, gasoline, and everything else. Sizes of packaging became smaller, yet prices became higher.

"Fake news" emerged, fooling millions of people who, over time, had grown to trust and believe that what they heard on the news was true. "Fake news creates stories and narratives that are false. People get together and create news that is fabricated and not vetted. There are no verifiable facts. We are not provided with sources of the information nor are there any reliable quotes. Many reporters lied and supported created news.

Many stories are propaganda, intentionally created to mislead the viewers. Sometimes the writer designs them as "click-bait," that the writer profits from the number of people who click on the story on their cell phones or computers. The content aims to attract attention and encourage readers to click on their website links, so they get paid for the number of clicks. Others are stories designed to mislead listeners into believing false narratives to influence their thinking and support their agendas.

This is a severe problem. I do not know what to believe because much of the news is designed to discredit opposing political views. They wish to cast doubt on the credibility of their opponents. It is also created to influence people about controversial issues to influence viewers in one way or another. This is terrible for our country and for the world. We used to watch news that was real news. Now we do not know what to believe as so many have been caught up in lies and fabricated stories that later proved to be false.

You cannot even trust "fact-checking" as many fabricators are also fact-checkers to make people think that something untrue is

117

true. It has gotten so bad that now we do not know what to believe unless we see it before our eyes.

It has reached a point where news is so untrustworthy that we must do two things:

One. Limit news to ten minutes in the morning, just to see if there was a terrorist attack or something true. Once we have the few stories of the day, many of us have zero interest in listening to them talk about it all day long. Much of it is designed to scare people, as the goal is to control humankind.

Two. Begin listening to real news on websites that are not influenced by these evil people. I find several of them more trustworthy. We each need to do our own research and decide where we can find the truth about just what is going on, especially in our own country.

The news upsets many of us, but it is best not to spend much time on it.

OUR EXTERNAL IMAGE

We alone determine how others will feel about us. They can only judge us by observing our conduct and hearing what we have to say. They know if we are positive or negative, and they know where our hearts are. Everyone who knows us is watching and listening to us. They judge us whether they tell us or not.

Our external persona is a mirror image of ourselves within. How we think determines what we say and do. In other words, how we think and act creates our external image to others. People make opinions about us by our conduct and our speech. Subsequently, our conduct is manifested in the external world as the cause of our positive or negative external image to others.

If we fail to meditate and spend time with our internal selves, we are experiencing too much of the external world. Much of our thinking comes from the effect that others have upon us. It is especially important to sit in the right classes and learn the right things. Even college professors often teach the wrong things, teaching their warped opinions instead of the material that is part of the class. At least, in this country, we usually have a choice. We can choose those that we want to teach us. We must be careful of what we absorb, which will reflect in our conduct and create the image we have of the outside world.

Here is something to give a lot of serious thought to:

"A positive self-image and healthy self-esteem are based on approval, acceptance, and recognition from others; but also, upon actual accomplishments, achievements and success upon the realistic self-confidence which ensues."

Abraham Maslow

FRIENDS DRIVE ME CRAZY

When we decide to transform and renew our minds, we just may have to change some friends who will not support us. You gave up getting "high," and your pot-smoking friends do not find you funny anymore and argue rather than support you. They want to get drunk every time they go out and cannot understand why you do not do that anymore.

"Be careful the environment you choose, for it will shape you; be careful the friends you choose, for you will become like them."

W. Clement Stone

If we have friends that do not like the new you, they are not really friends anyway. Find new friends. It would help you to join a bible-based church and make new friends there, before and after church, in the coffee room, or joining bible discussion groups. If we do, this will not only help us to get through our tough times, but it will lead to a calmer and happier life. It is amazing the results we feel when we stop continuously doing things that are bad for us. Good things begin to happen. We have better luck with our health, happiness and in our job. Just decide to stop doing wrong things with friends and watch how fast good things start happening to you.

That said, we must not allow others to offend us. Bounce off anything negative that they say. We rob ourselves of joy and happiness when others make us angry. Instead, we harbor bitterness and resentment in our hearts and in our minds. When a friend criticizes your changes, courteously say, "I do not wish to argue with you. You have a right to your opinions, and I have a right not to agree with them." I want to improve the quality of my life. In short, I want to grow up and continue to have fun, but without losing control.

Take the time to select one or two close good friends that will support you in how you want to lead your life.

"People look at the outward appearance, but the Lord looks at the heart."

1 Samuel 16:7

That is exactly what we should look for in a friend with a good and loving heart. Whether one is short, tall, fat, skinny, or of any

120

race, color, or creed, none of these are as important as choosing a friend. A good friend has a good heart and will stand behind you with support, especially when facing challenging times. A good friend has absolutely nothing to do with their exterior appearance. Examine what is in their heart and soul.

BULLIED

The word bully was derived from the Middle-Dutch word "boele," which means lover or sweetheart. It eventually took on the opposite meaning of anyone who exerted physical or mental abuse on those they think they can get away from it. A bully enjoys browbeating people with cruel, blustering, insulting, and even unwanted sexual advances. Unfortunately, many people are bullied, especially children. However, many adults are bullied as well. Sometimes it is a woman by her husband or a girl by her boyfriend. Even bad bosses can be bullies, which is not how professionally trained managers are supposed to act.

Some ruffian teen boys love to torment someone smaller and weaker than them. Others tease a student who has a physical problem. They never stop to think how badly they can damage these victims, some even committing suicide. Some women, especially drug addicts, turn to prostitution and end up with a pimp who not only verbally abuses them but beats them for the fun of it.

"I got made fun of constantly in high school. That's what built my character. That's what makes you who you are. When you get made fun of, when people point out your weakness, that's just another opportunity for you to rise above."

Zac Efron

121

If you are bullied, you should report this action to as many people as possible until it is stopped. If your child or anyone you know is bullied, you should take action to get the behavior stopped. If a school fails to act, call the police or the superintendent of schools. Just do not stand down and let this extremely dangerous and damaging conduct continue.

Scripture tells us to control how we feel after someone bullies us. God wants us to take refuge when we are oppressed. Just take refuge in Jesus and call upon Him for help. Vengeance is God's. Those that bully will be punished. No one gets away with hurting others.

"Get rid of all bitterness, rage, and anger, brawling and slander, along with every form of malice. Be kind and compassionate to one another, forgiving each other, just as in Christ God forgave you."

Ephesians 4:31

Chapter 10

FINANCIAL PROBLEMS

I WENT BANKRUPT

Bankruptcy is a tough problem to have to face. Many millionaires went bankrupt at least once or had to bankrupt one of their companies. I had to go bankrupt once over several huge problems that I could not control or change. It was a lesson I never forgot, but I worked day and night to make it back.

We must do all we can to avoid bankruptcy because it is a huge blemish and takes a long time to clean one's credit. Before we declare bankruptcy, we normally endure a couple of years of fighting to stay afloat. It is tough. We work extra hours, desperately trying to get the money we need to pay our bills. We must, at minimum, send all creditors something each month, with a letter of explanation.

We even start selling our possessions to pay bills. Many of us lose our homes and must move out after the painful repossessions and evictions begin. Some lose everything they own in a fire or massive storm that takes away everything. Most of us try extremely hard to avoid bankruptcy, as it can lead to desperation, nervous outbursts, and extreme anxiety.

For those going down with a business, it is a slow painful death. Our supply houses expect cash deliveries and, eventually, we cannot get anything we need to continue. The delinquent payments eventually lower our credit report to unacceptable levels. Then stores and everyone refuse to give credit. We realize we lost and need to start over. There were no stones left unturned. All has failed; the only alternative is to claim bankruptcy and start over.

We may have to find a new job or even a new career. At first, we may have to take any job and slowly work ourselves back into the field of work that we enjoy doing.

We must exercise perseverance and aggressively seek reasonable goals to start and then slowly increase them as the money starts to build. However, when we get credit next time, we must not overuse the card. Keep it to a budget that we can pay on time.

"To overcome failure, we must exercise perseverance, aggressively seeking worthy goals, defeating all obstacles, regardless of any previous failures."

Matt Jordan

Immediately after bankruptcy, we must start to rebuild credit in a small way. Sometimes the best thing to do is to buy a prepaid credit card. It can be small, like just $200. But it should be used every month, even for small purchases that should be paid immediately. Gradually, our credit improves and eventually gets clean, and everything negative will be wiped out. It takes years to rebuild a clean credit report, but time flies, and you will start getting credit sooner than you think.

During the terrible tough time of moving into bankruptcy, it helps to turn to God. Life here on earth is short and extremely fast.

"The things which are seen are temporary, but the things which are not seen are eternal."

2 Corinthians 4:18

I LOST MY MONEY GAMBLING

Gambling can quickly become an addiction that is called pathological or compulsive gambling. Some call it a gambling disorder. It is an impulse-control disorder because one loses control of the temptation to gamble. The addict continues to gamble, even when the consequences happen to loved ones.

Thank God, I never was much of a gambler. Gambling is like drugs or alcohol; without control, it will lead to addiction. But I knew several gambling addicts are present from all levels of society as it starts out fun. Let us assume that you win a couple of hundred dollars at the track or on a table at a casino. But the hunger grows to win increasingly. Gamblers bet on casino tables, slots, sports, scratch cards, racetracks, and worse yet, online, where the winning percentages for the house may be the highest of all places to gamble.

"It's better to own the casino than being the gambler in the casino."

Tina Larsson

Gambling has destroyed many marriages, as some keep betting higher and higher limits, trying to win back their losses. Gambling addicts know the consequences and that the odds are all against them. Eventually, they even realize they cannot afford to lose any

125

more money. Unfortunately, these people often end up losing their homes and spouses as their debts climb to unmanageable levels. Some even steal money to gamble as they become desperate to regain their losses. Others are falsely led to believe that one can get rich by gambling. The Bible teaches us that there is no good in gaining the entire world and losing our souls. Even when a gambler wins big, it is not money that he will keep. He will lose it one day because it was not earned with good demanding work. Just as an alcoholic cannot take even one drink, the gambler cannot make even one bet. The temptation must be avoided, and the addict must think about the consequences.

Like all addictions, healing is a long and tough road.

Support is necessary.

I LOST MY JOB

Undoubtedly, losing a job is cause for both concern and being upset. But consider: why did you lose it? Were you trying to do work that you hated to do? I have said this before, 80% of Americans hate their job because they are not within the field of work that God created them to do.

Now, if you did love your job but were downsized through no fault of your own, the situation is a little different. Either way, you must do the same thing. You must analyze just what field of work the Lord created you to do. Music? Teaching? Science? Medicine? Whatever field you choose, there are many distinct types of work to choose from. For example, if it is the medical field, you can become a doctor, nurse, hospital worker, testing lab, doctor assistant, and many others. If it is the field of music, you can perform, write, conduct, teach, or arrange. There are also many other jobs. Once you are sure you are seeking a job within the field you were created to do, you must first get the proper education to do it and then get some experience working under someone who can train you.

If you lose your job, you still have a full-time job. Your job is to spend 8 hours a day working on your resume, job searching, visiting companies, doing interviews, sending out letters, and keeping busy all day. Do not sit around waiting for someone to call you. You will feel better keeping busy than wallowing in losing your job, regardless of why you lost it. It was just meant to be, and there is something better for you to do.

"I never regretted turning down anything; I never regretted losing a job because I always felt something else was out there."

Carol Burnett

Do not fear job interviews. Just go there with a resume and be yourself. Do not try to be what you think they want you to be. Be sure you are applying for a job you love. Then go there, smartly dressed, and just be yourself. Remember your strengths, and with confidence and enthusiasm, you will do fine at the interview. I have performed hundreds of interviews over the last forty-plus years. Whenever I interviewed anyone for a job, the first thing I always tried to do was to calm the person down. I can tell when they came in nervous or spurting out "canned" rehearsed lines, trying too hard to impress.

I do think it is nice to dress up clean and to look nice for an interview. In fact, failure to groom oneself and going in looking very sloppy makes a negative impression. "We never get a second chance to make a first impression. This is our chance to impress in the right manner, and we should not blow the opportunity.

127

Bringing an impressive list of schools and jobs and reference letters will help.

I always liked to see some typed letters of reference, especially on letterheads. I am going to go against protocol here and add this. I think adding the statement at the bottom of your resume, "references upon request," is ridiculous. References are always helpful. Why should any manager have to ask for them? Do we really think that they will ask everyone they interview for references? Would it not be better if they conveniently had ours? I loved it when someone handed me some letters of reference to look through.

It is also wise to bring in samples of your work. For example, if you are an architect, you should bring drawings of things you have done with you and ask to show them, and talk about them the same way you would show them and talk about them to someone close to you. We do want to make an impression. We just do not want to make a bad impression, and we all know "we do not get a second chance to make a first impression."

We can do that by looking well-groomed and dressed, like a professional, and delivering professional-looking paperwork. Then we should just be ourselves and talk the same way we would talk to a relative or friend. Our mission is to make the interviewer enjoy our company and believe that we are not only capable but also someone who would make for a desirable employee.

Chapter 11

MAKING THINGS BETTER

AFTER BEING KNOCKED DOWN

What do you do if you are knocked down so badly that you do not want to get up? A close loved one died, and you feel you cannot live without them. Or you lost your job, went bankrupt, or went through some other trauma that knocked you down. In such cases, we feel that life is over for us. We lost our desire to live, believing that life will never be the same.

Just understand that the devil wants you to stay down. He is not going to help you get up. If we lose a close loved one, a spouse, parents, sibling, or child, we have a right to cry, mourn, and feel depressed and sad.

But for how long?

Certainly not over a year.

We must do what that loved one would want us to do. We do not have to stay on the ground and in the pits. We must get back up and get on with our lives. Remember that you have not reached your destiny yet. If you failed to plan, you planned to fail. It is like

129

falling off a horse. What do they say if someone falls off a horse? "Get back on the horse, or you may never do that again."

So, something bad has happened. That happens to us all. Take the time to adjust to it, but you must get back up – so set new goals and get busy conducting your purpose in life. You are not done yet. Happiness, health, and success can be yours. Stay close to God when you are knocked down, and tell Him you cannot do this without him.

"Bring our concerns to Him to meet our needs and give peace."

Philippians 4:6

JUST KEEP CHOPPING

If one must chop down a tall and wide tree, the task begins with the first swing. Then you keep chopping away at it. Eventually, with perseverance and patience, the tree falls. That is what we must do when we are going through a tough period of tough times. We must keep chopping away, doing something every day that makes us feel better. It is step by step, with patience and determination to make things better.

"Be strong and of good courage. Do not fear and be afraid."

Deuteronomy 31:6

The way we get through a tough impossible problem is to chip away at it, one chop at a time, step by step. Make a checklist and work your way through it, checking off each step as you complete it. Any long task must be broken down one step at a time with courage. The journey begins with the first step. Sometimes that first step is the hardest to do, and we procrastinate it for days, even weeks. Once you take that step, others follow much easier.

Do not let obstacles and hindrances get in your way. Work your way through them. Get help if needed and then resume the positive steps up the ladder.

"Believe you can, and you're halfway there."

Theodore Roosevelt

OVERCOMING DOUBT & UNBELIEF

We must remove all doubt when we are waiting for our prayers to be answered. If we have any disbelief, healing will never work. Doubt is considered "unbelief." If one says, "well, I am not sure this will work, but I am going up to the altar at the next church service and ask to be prayed for a healing." With that attitude, I assure you that healing will never come.

"But let him ask in faith, with no doubting, for the one who doubts is like a wave of the sea that is driven and tossed by the wind."

James 1:6

We must instead believe before when we pray for healing. Also, when we are prayed for by others, we must believe that we already have the healing. We must picture ourselves well and do all the normal things we used to do. This is true even for a life-threatening illness. We must keep all faith and not worry, which is the opposite of faith.

"Inaction breeds doubt and fear. Action breeds confidence and courage."

Dale Carnegie

LAYING HANDS FOR HEALING

We know that we all are the temple of God and that God's Spirit lives within born-again Christians. Our spirit has unlimited power, but as I have said, our level of consciousness and our inner power is affected by many factors, especially by our levels of stress.

I like Andrew Wommack's explanation of how laying hands on someone can heal them from sickness. He compared it to using someone's car to jump-start our car when we find the battery dead, and the car will not start. The power from the car that has a strong battery is shifted to the car with the dead battery, so the car starts.

We all have the power to lay hands on the sick and transfer the power of God through us to the person who is sick. It is not the hand of the person that heals; it is God who is doing the healing through our hands. Many Christians have healed many ill people by laying hands on them.

Numerous people have been healed this way. However, numerous people have not been healed when someone lays hands on them because of their unbelief. Sometimes when we pray for healing, or others pray for us, we must wait for the healing to manifest. We must fully believe it is coming. The prayer is like planting a seed. It takes time for the ground to take that seed and grow it into fruits, vegetables, or whatever was planted. A farmer

132

must be patient. So must one who has prayed for healing. During the period of waiting, the risk is that some doubt will arise. That is a huge mistake. If we do that, we do not allow the healing to manifest at God's timing. It is like a football player running in an entire accessible area, giving up, and sitting down. The result, of course, would be no touchdown. Do not give up while in the period of manifestation. Let the seeds germinate and grow to full blossom.

Often, God works through others. When we are sick, we must go to a doctor and get a diagnosis. Then we must get the medication and surgery before the healing is manifested. Help God out here. When you get sick, do not just pray. Allow God to send you to wherever you must go to get this healing to manifest.

We have the power to plant a healing seed ourselves. We can command the following:

"I take authority over my (Problem, illness.) and I speak directly to it to leave me now in the name of Jesus. Go now!"

BREATHING TECHNIQUES

Because breathing is so important for stress and anxiety relief and even for healing, I am going to spend more time on this segment. We all must know the dangers of "shallow breathing" and the benefits of deep breathing. I also will give you some of the breathing exercises I find immensely helpful.

When we are upset, we all have heard someone advise us, "take a deep breath." Breathing is especially important to the health of the body, which needs a lot of oxygen. It is important to spend time every day focusing on your breathing to help you to stay healthy.

Since I began studying breathing techniques many years ago, I started watching how people breathe and saw that many of them incorrectly "shallow breathe." Shallow breathing denies the body adequate fresh oxygen. You correct this by learning how to fill the lungs with air to give the body more energy and vitality.

Shallow breathing creates tension in the body and can lead to tough times because we are leaving dead air in the lungs, thus denying the body adequate fresh oxygen. The dangers are that we can build high anxiety, panic attacks, fatigue, and dry mouth. This can even lead to serious respiratory problems like cardiovascular disease and even heart attacks. We need to correct this by learning how to fill the lungs with deep breathing to provide more oxygen to the body, as well as more energy and vitality.

Other benefits include pain relief, improved immunity, energy, better digestion, improved posture, pain relief, and lower blood pressure. It will help us to relax and decrease the release of the stress hormone Cortisol, which causes insomnia.

"Deep breathing brings deep thinking, and shallow breathing brings shallow thinking."

Elsie Lincoln Benedict

It is beneficial to practice breathing techniques both when we wake up and when we go to bed to get our body breathing longer and healthier breaths. There are several breathing techniques we can use to release stress

Here are the ones that I personally use.

DIAPHRAGM BREATHING

There are various breathing techniques that one can use to take deeper beneficial breaths. Certainly, "diaphragm (belly) breathing" is where one should start, taking deep breaths, starting with the belly, and filling the lower lungs.

Some try to train this form of breathing by strapping a tight belt around the chest so that one cannot breathe from the upper lungs. I disagree with this because you cannot totally fill your lungs if you have a belt strapped around your chest. It is best to fill the lower lungs with the belly as far as you can go and then fill the upper portion of the lungs using the chest.

You start with the belly for about five counts and then use two more counts to raise the chest and finish filling the lungs with air. Take at least seven seconds to complete this process. Then, it is good to hold your breath for around four counts. Then take seven counts to let the breath completely out.

RAPID BREATHING

Rapid breathing can be done through the mouth and or the nose. Some feel that we should not breathe through the mouth, so you may prefer to use the nose. Therefore, this form of breathing does help to build our force and energy.

It is effective to increase oxygen to help us to wake up and for cleansing the sinus passages. This is the first kind of breathing that I do soon after I wake up and do the things you read in my morning routine. If we have problems with the sinuses and eyes and have a little sinus headache, rapid breathing can help to clear these. It also will create heat within the body. If we have a lot of mucus in the air passages or feel tension and blockages in the chest, it is helpful to breathe quickly. Breathing quickly is also a fast way to release stress or anger when involved in a negative situation.

I use rapid breathing through the nose. We should breathe from the lower abdomen using our diaphragm and then fill up the chest with air. The breaths are short, rapid, and strong. We use the lungs as a pump to create pressure. We remove waste as we expel the air from the air passages, from the lungs up through the nostrils. Pick your own number of times. I do these 30 to 40 times.

SLOW DIAPHRAGM BREATHING

Breaths should be taken slowly, easily, and fully. We must use the diaphragm to get as much air in as possible. I start out with a four-count in, hold four, release with a four-count and then hold the breath again for four. I do this several times. Then I move up to five counts for each, then six, seven, until I can get up to a twelve count. I try to get soft hissing, like the sound of the ocean. I purse my lips to make the sound while narrowing the back of my throat as if whispering to someone. This helps to improve concentration, diminish distractions, and create heat in the body.

I have COPD, Chronic Obstructive Pulmonary Disease. When I first wake up, I cough if I breathe in too much air, so I must start with a low count of four. This will be true for all of you that have any kind of a problem with your lungs. However, those of you that have healthy lungs can start with a larger number, as you can do.

This technique also helps to clear our nasal passages with the force of our breath. Remember the nose filters the air, so it is best to breathe in from our nose. It is good for allergy relief and

136

invigorates and creates heat in the body. In addition, it will help remove stress and wake up in the morning.

I once saw someone talking about belly breathing on a doctor's show, and he suggested that you strap a belt around your chest to breathe only from the belly. I do not use a strap. I simply fill up with air as far as I can with the belly, but I find that you can get more air in if you finish filling your upper lungs by expanding your chest. Otherwise, chances are you are not totally filling up your lungs totally with air if you are using a strap.

ALTERNATE NOSTRIL BREATHING

I like using this form of breathing also to help open my sinus passages when they feel clogged when waking up. I also like to use it to calm my anxiety and regain clear thinking when it appears to be "foggy" at times. This form of breathing will calm me down if I get angry or stressed over something.

Here is how you perform this technique. You hold your right hand up, curled around your nose. Then place your thumb next to your right nostril and your ring finger by your left nostril. You close the right nostril by pressing gently against it with your thumb and inhale through the left nostril. The breath should be slow, steady, and full.

We then close the left nostril by pressing against it with the ring finger and open the right nostril by relaxing the thumb and exhaling fully and slowly. Then we alternate by inhaling through the right nostril. We close it and then exhale through the left nostril. In short, inhale through the left and exhale through the right. Then, inhale through the right, and exhale through the left. Continue this at least seven times.

137

When we breathe through one nostril at a time and out through the other nostril, we are balancing breath. In doing so, we balance our left and right brains and nervous systems.

ANALYZING OUR STRENGTH

I once heard something in a church sermon that I felt was extremely important. We have all heard, "A chain is as strong as its weakest link." Perhaps we should also consider that "We are as strong as our weakest link." What is our weakest link? We must identify whatever it is and replace it with a strong link.

Is our weak link an addiction to alcohol, drugs, or whatever? Is it that we watch television ten hours a day? Or must we drink coffee and eat sugar all day long to stay awake? Is it that we only sleep three or four hours a night? Is it that we must be shopping in stores or on the Internet every single day or night? Is it an illness that we take medications to simply mask the real core reason of the problem and do nothing to heal it? Of course, none of these are good for us and will bring us into unnecessarily demanding times. It helps our strength to grow when we analyze and remove our weaknesses. You may be different from those examples above.

"Be on your guard; stand firm in the faith; be courageous; be strong."

1 Corinthians 16:13

If we feel weak all the time, we must find out why. There must be a mental or a physical problem that we must take the time to identify and heal. Usually, this will require us to see a doctor, natural healer, or psychologist to get help solving the issue.

138

It is urgent for us during times in our life when we feel weak to find out why, solve the problem, get to the gym, and get strong again. Our mind has a direct relationship with our body.

"Weak mind; weak body. Weak body; weak mind."

Matt Jordan

TURN NEGATIVES INTO POSITIVES

Let us think about some negative feelings that we can turn into positives. Look at the list below to get an idea of what this exercise can do to help you become more positive.

Sadness to Happiness

Depression to Elation

Fatigue to Energetic

Weakness to Strength

Impatience to Patience

Worry to Confidence

Lack of common sense to Wisdom

Most of us, no doubt, would prefer to have the positive things listed above rather than the negative alternatives. No one likes to feel sad. When this feeling arises, ask yourself, "what can I do to feel happy? Perhaps put a comedy on television that will make you laugh. Laughter is great for healing many things, including certain illnesses.

The other possibility is that we can change what we are thinking. For example, if we are thinking about someone we read in the news who passed away, we should think about a friend who had a baby instead. Look at the pictures and feel happy doing so. Whatever you choose to think about, make it something you love and enjoy. Think about happy things. Perhaps put on your favorite music. Dance all by yourself. It is fun. Many of us do it.

If we are feeling depressed, once again, we need to do or think of things that bring us elation. There was a great vacation we went on. Find some photos from that vacation, look at them, and feel the joy you felt when you took them.

If we feel tired, we need to take a nap as soon as possible. Also, if we meditate upon a word we love, we can feel like we had some sleep. But we must meditate on the word for at least twenty minutes.

If our body feels weak, then we should go to the gym or for a walk. Exercise can give us just the lift we need to feel more energetic. However, do not turn to coffee and energy drinks because they are acidic and will make you sick in time.

If we are impatient, we begin thinking or doing things that will upset us. Impatience can set in if we are missing all the green lights or standing in all the slowest lines. When impatient, we risk dropping things, swearing, or fighting with people. We act foolishly and need to do something to turn our impatience into patience.

The best thing to do in these situations is to rest your mind. Instead of getting angry at the traffic lights or at the person in line who is taking forever, think about some happy things to do that will make you feel more patient. Or meditate thinking over and over one word that will calm you, like love, gentle, Jesus, roses, or whatever you love.

If we are feeling worried, we should analyze what we are worrying about. Take out a pen and paper and begin listing positive things you can plan to turn the worry into confidence.

If we are making a lot of bad decisions, chances are that we lack common sense, and we need to develop wisdom. I mentioned that wisdom comes with age. Find an older person you both like and respect and set up a time to talk to them and listen to their advice. We must learn wisdom.

Try listing some things you feel are negative and work out what you can do to turn these into positives.

Often, terrible things happen in life. My advice has always been to find a way to turn a negative into a positive. That is where the expression "Every cloud has a silver lining" comes from." We must work to find some good in the situation we can develop into positives.

Part Three

AVOIDING BAD TIMES

Chapter 12

THE FRUITS OF THE SPIRIT

WHAT ARE THE FRUITS OF SPIRIT?

We all go through tough times that we must conquer. They are simply different problems that happen to each of us at various times. There are several solutions that we will discuss to help us to overcome them. However, none are more important than to understand, develop and demonstrate in our conduct, the "Fruits of the Spirit."

These are characteristics that we all must feel and practice in the daily living of our lives. They are love, joy, peace, patience, kindness, goodness, gentleness, forgiveness, faithlessness, and self-control. Such a Spirit-controlled life will please God because it bears the "Fruits of the Spirit."

When we are not practicing the fruits of the spirit, we will feel the opposites, hatred, pain, sadness, calamity, impatience, meanness, crudeness, mercilessness, unfaithfulness, and total lack of control. God will not be in our lives. While His Spirit lives in all of us, we will bury it with all this negativity.

"The moment a person believes in Jesus through faith, they receive the Holy Spirit."

Galatians 3:2

In practicing these characteristics, we demonstrate the sanctification that we experience in our hearts. When those who believe in Jesus release these characteristics, others will want to do this as well. It makes others feel better when we act like Christians.

"We live by the Spirit, let us keep in step with the Spirit. Let us not become conceited, provoking, and envying each other."

Galatians 5:25

We will examine each of these fruits. It would be a clever idea to take notes and develop a plan, especially for the characteristics within which you do not feel. Others may have them all, and if you do, you are an exception. However, if you do feel you have them all, you should objectively ask someone you live with what they think. Ask them if they feel that you are demonstrating these fruits in your daily life. They may say that they do not see these in you. If not, you must not get angry at them, but instead, practice each of the characteristics.

Let us look at each of the "fruits of spirit," and objectively analyze whether we are emulating all of these, or not. I do not think that priests, reverends, rabbis, or even the pope emulate these as well as Jesus.

LOVE

Many do not feel love for anyone. Yet they wonder why they are not loved. The truth is, we must earn the love of others. No one loves a sour, negative, complaining, nasty person.

We must give others love to get love in return. Do we say, "I love you" often enough or at all? Better yet, do we show our love for others by acting towards them?

"Love must be sincere. Hate what is evil; cling to what is good. Be devoted to one another in love. Honor one another above yourselves."

Romans 12:9

There are many kinds of love available to us.

"What does love like? It has the hands to help others. It has the feet to hasten to the poor and needy. It has eyes to see misery and want. It has the ears to hear the sighs and sorrows of men. That is what love looks like."

Augustine

We can love God and show our love for Him by thanking Him for all that we have and trying to avoid breaking His commandments.

We can love our church, our pastor, and our fellow members.

We can love people around us, greeting them and showing them our love and respect.

We can love our parents, children and all our relatives.

We can love our friends.

We can love music, art, architecture, and all we see and hear.

We can love our country.

We can love the beautiful nature, the flowers, trees, and plants.

Then there is the difference between the love for all the above and "being in love" with our spouse.

"Let love and faithfulness never leave you; bind them around your neck, write them on the tablet of your heart."

Proverbs 3:3

We all know, if we live a life without love, it is a sad way to live. The bible teaches us that without love, we have nothing. We must give it away freely and often if we want to receive it.

"Love each other deeply because love covers over a multitude of sins."

1 Peter 4:8

JOY

Joy is a feeling of comfort, confidence, pleasure, and tranquility. I will write more about this later in the book, in more detail. It is difficult to feel joy in times of great sadness. I promise you, after reading this book, if you apply the informative suggestions, you will always feel joy no matter what is going on around you.

Even the terrible feeling that we have when we lose a loved one, we all feel joy if we say close to God and feel His love. He will never abandon or forsake us. He does not sleep or leave us alone. He lives within each of us and comforts us when we are sad.

146

It is like we all have our own individual God who is listening to our prayers and grants us peace when we ask for it.

"Count it all joy, my brothers when you meet trials of various kinds, for you know that the testing of your faith produces steadfastness."

James 1:2

So, when you are down, please thinking about this promise of God, no matter what or how difficult your problem is. You can feel joy, knowing you are saved, and you are going to heaven, which I describe later in the book.

"Joy is the infallible sign of the presence of God."

Pierre Teilhard de Chardin

PEACE

The feeling of peace is available to us. It requires us to control anxiety, which I will cover. We should never allow our hearts to be troubled to the point of only feeling turmoil. It takes control of all the suggestions I have given you in this book, much of which I had to learn the hard way, living in the school of hard knocks.

We must take the time to feel peace – a state of tranquility. Sometimes, if the circumstance around us is so turbulent, we must get away to be alone to feel the joy of peace.

"You have peace when you make it with yourself."

Mitch Albom

We can sit in a church and pray to find peace. Or, we can go near water, or nature, to meditate and release excess stress and anxiety.

147

Peace is not always available to us if we are living in an unhealthy relationship. We must do one of two things. Correct and save the relationship or end it. No matter what our circumstances are, we must work to feel peace.

"I have told you these things, so that in me you may have peace. In this world, you will have trouble. But take heart! I have overcome the world."

John 16:33

PATIENCE

"Wait for the Lord; be strong and take heart and wait for the Lord."

Psalm 27:14

Oh my, how I struggle with this one – I have done so all my life. But I now at least know that being impatient is one of the most hurtful things that we can do to others and ourselves. I still make mistakes, but I am aware of them, and I attempt to avoid them. Things happen that will try our patience every day. Life is not easy for any of us, but it can be beautiful if we do the right things to enjoy it.

"Be completely humble and gentle; be patient, bearing with one another in love."

Ephesians 4:2

We pick the wrong line in a bank or store and all the others move faster, so we get grumpy and sometimes, even downright nasty. We hit every red light. There is an accident on a highway, and we sit, bumper to bumper in our car wondering what is wrong

148

ahead of us. One practicing patience, someone long-suffering, will tolerate the attacks of others without being offended.

Impatience is a negative characteristic many of us have struggled through. It happens increasingly, especially when we are allowing ourselves to drop in our level of consciousness.

At higher levels, we develop patience which happens with sufficient sleep, focused breathing, exercise, meditation, and prayer. When suffering from anxiety, impatience is soon to follow. When impatient, we doubt the outcome of the situation that we want to happen sooner rather than later. When Patient, we are slow to anger, confident in our ability to create a positive outcome of whatever we are waiting for, and we are doing all that we can.

"Patience is the best remedy for every trouble."

Plautus

One of the things I try to do during these times I feel impatient is to take a deep breath, meditate and pray. When we think about why many of our problems have happened, we often find that the problem was caused by our lack of patience, causing us to mushroom the problem to be much larger than it was.

"Impatience turns an ague (a shivering chill) into a fever, a fever to the plague, fear into despair, anger into rage, loss into madness, and sorrow into frenzy."

Jeremy Taylor

149

KINDNESS

Kindness requires us to be generously friendly and considerate of others. When we are angry with someone, it is difficult to be kind to them. We all fail to be kind to everyone, all the time. It is not easy for everyone, including me. However, we improve the quality of our own lives when we take the time to help the lives of others, giving them genuine acts of kindness and compassion.

"Carry out a random act of kindness, with no expectation of reward, safe in the knowledge that one day someone might do the same for you."

Princess Diana

We must be kind to all, regardless of the differences in politics, religion, or any difference in opinions. Whether we act kind or nasty will reveal the goodness or badness within our hearts. Kindness requires patience and listening to others, even if we hate what they are saying to us. Before we respond, we must give them the courtesy of hearing them out, listening to all they say because they just might be right.

"Be kind and compassionate to one another, forgiving each other, just as in Christ God forgave you."

Ephesians 4:32

150

GOODNESS

"Lord, do good to those who are good, to those who are upright in heart."

Psalm 125:4-5

Goodness is a characteristic of being moral, virtuous, and avoiding evil. But when the world is so gray, how do we know where we walk? Good or evil. Black or white. God lives within our heart and soul. He knows what we have done and will do. But what about us?

It is quite simple, one who appears good to others does not practice wrongful conduct, even if it is at the expense of their net worth or their notoriety. God expects us to read the rules and laws of the Bible and practice them daily because it helps us understand our place in the world morally. We all must try to be as good as we can, at least, most of the time. It helps for others to see goodness in us when we practice the Fruits of the Spirit, which blends in perfectness.

Goodness is a characteristic of being moral, virtuous, and avoiding evil. Santa knows whether we have been "bad or good" and God knows all that we think and all that we do. Did the writer of the quote about Santa think he was writing about God?

One who appears good to others does not practice wrongful conduct, even if it is at the expense of their net worth or their notoriety. God expects us to read the rules and laws of the bible and practice them daily. We all must try to be as good as we can, at least, most of the time. It helps others to see goodness in us when we practice the Fruits of the Spirit, which blends in perfectness.

151

"Be the reason someone smiles. Be the reason someone feels loved and believes in the goodness in people."

Roy T. Bennett

"Lord, do good to those who are good, to those who are upright in heart."

Psalm 125:4-5

"I have told you these things so that in me you may have peace. In this world, you will have trouble. But take heart! I have overcome the world."

John 16:33

GENTLENESS

It is prudent to avoid speaking loudly to a person who has done or said something that is annoying to us. Obeying the Golden Rule requires us to be tender and kind when we speak to others, even if we are angry with them. This is not easy; we all know that. It is a quality to be tolerant and respective of others. We should not put ourselves up high on a pedestal. We should speak to a truck driver the same way we speak to a multi-millionaire.

"In the long run, the sharpest weapon of all is a kind and gentle spirit."

Anne Frank

A gentle person will act mild in behavior, rather than become angry in situations that are not comfortable. The person is courteous rather than vindictive, yielding to others for the sake of obeying the laws of God.

152

"I am gentle and humble of heart."

Mathew 11:29

There is power in gentleness as it gets us positive results. It is not a sign of weakness at all. We need to find a tactful way to make a point and not make an enemy. This may require us to think first when we know we are going to say something that could sound harsh.

FORGIVENESS

Many of us know someone that committed something so bad, we cannot even think of forgiveness. There can be terrible acts committed against us or someone we love. Such acts just cannot be forgiven. A few examples could be among the following:

Your dad viciously beat you when you were a child.

Your dad used to beat up your mom.

Someone stole all your money.

Someone abused your spouse.

Your spouse cheated on you.

Your addict child stole and sold all your valuables.

Someone set you up to look bad and stole your promotion.

There are many other examples of offenses that may have occurred that you considered so bad, that you cannot forgive. But here is the problem when you do not forgive. God will not forgive us if we do not forgive others. This is not my opinion; this is in the bible.

153

"If we do not forgive others for their trespasses, God will not forgive us for our trespasses."

Matthew 16:15

God will forgive that person if they confess Jesus as their savior and repent, but not forgive us. Does this seem fair? This is so hard to do; it may take numerous attempts on our part before we can clear our minds by truly forgiving. The bible also addressed this as follows:

"Lord, how often shall my brother sin against me, and I forgive him? As many as seven times?" Jesus said to him, "I do not say to you seven times, but seventy times seven."

Matthew 18:21, 22.

What this is saying is that God knows it often is difficult to forgive a terrible person. We must do this even if it takes us 149 times or more! We must do it, over and over, as many times as necessary, until we truly forgive the terrible acts.

What happens to us if we do not? I am not sure what God would do because of breaking His word. In a way, He lets us feel the consequences of unforgiveness. We will dash out the punishment to ourselves. We will let this harbor within our minds, negatively affecting our whole life. We will never reach anywhere near the highest level of consciousness. We will never fully feel love, joy, peace, kindness, goodness, faithfulness, and gentleness – we will not fully be able to use self-control.

Instead, we will feel hatred, sadness, anxiety, meanness, harshness, vengeance, coldness, depression, and much more.

What does that mean for our health, happiness, and success?

154

FAITHFULNESS

Faith is the feeling of complete trust or confidence in someone or something. Some have full and infinite faith in God, spiritual belief without proof. It is difficult to use self-control if we do not have full faith and faithfulness.

"Faith is the way we get above fears we feel in bad times."

Matt Jordan

"Since then, you have been raised with Christ, set your hearts on things above."

Colossians 3:1

Faithfulness is a characteristic of having faith in God or a spouse, friend, boss, politician, or whoever. One with faithfulness has the quality of being true to one's commitments to complete the things pledged to do. God, Himself has faithfulness because He is keeping all his promises in His word. We must practice faithfulness to God. This requires us to live our life in accordance with God's laws and His will. This is difficult for us to do all the time. But we must always try to use self-control not just while in church on Sunday but every day. Having faith and being obedient to God's laws does not mean occasionally doing so on Sundays. Having faith requires us to believe in things "unseen," and not in what we see all around us.

"Faithfulness is our business; fruitfulness is an issue that we must be content to leave with God."

J. I. Packer

It means it will affect our health and bring on sickness. We cannot be happy and sad at the same time. It also will hinder our level of success, so we never fully succeed in our job or business.

155

Folks, this may be the hardest thing you have to do to get through tough times – forgiving someone you wish would die.

SELF-CONTROL

Sometimes in life, we get so upset, we just lose it. We feel baffled and unable to think or speak clearly. We lose control over what we do, unable to not only understand but unable to control what we say or do.

"Better a patient person than a warrior, one with self-control than one who takes a city."

Proverbs 16:32

We must be careful when we lose control not to offend others with nasty behavior. When we are out of control, we must take immediate steps to regain control. Use the tools from this book, deep breathing, meditation, prayer, and stretching. We do not want to take our frustrations out at the expense of others. Self- control means more than just letting out steam or mistreating those around us.

It means to count to ten when we feel we are ready to deliver an outburst of anger and reply with a soft answer. It also means controlling how much we eat and what we eat to control our health and weight. It means not watching television for hours every day. It means not stopping in bars after work every night for drinks. It means not over doing anything, so we do and use things in moderation.

It means that we always should obey the golden rule and say it the way we would want it said to us. Not all of us can control ourselves, our emotions, our desire, and our conduct. We must

156

always keep in mind that our thoughts lead us to our actions, which lead us to our habits, which lead us to a lifestyle, which takes us to our final destiny. If we lack self-control all the time, what do you think our destiny would be?

"I cannot trust a man to control others who cannot control himself."

Robert E. Lee

Chapter 13

HOW TO FIGHT

TEMPTATION

ORIGINAL SIN

"...For we all have sinned and fall short of the glory of God."

Romans 3:23

We understand that there is only one God, who created everyone and everything, everywhere. He is manifested in His Holy Trinity of God the Father, God the Son, and God the Holy Spirit. The origination of sin goes back to God's creation of human beings, the first two human beings, Adam, and Eve.

They both were born with a perfect mind, body, and spirit, completely one with God. Their Spirit was full, innocent, and alive. However, when they broke the rule of God and ate from the forbidden apple tree, they were no longer perfect and free from sin.

They became carnal, living in the "flesh." They were naked before and after they sinned. However, they became aware of their nakedness after sinning and turned to cover their sexuality.

158

Because of their sin, and we all are descendants of Adam and Eve, we all were born with original sin.

"Behold, I was brought forth in iniquity, and in sin did my mother conceive me."

Psalm 51:5

Being born with original sin does not give us the excuse to live a sinful life. When we accept Jesus as our Lord and Savior, we need to repent. Repentance requires us to change our ways. We need to better control what we think and subsequently, what we do or say.

"Original sin is the only doctrine that's been empirically validated by 2,000 years of human history."

Gilbert K. Chesterton

TEMPTATION

Temptation starts in mind. We think of doing something that we should not do that is unwise and wrong. Sometimes the temptation is to buy something we really do not need or cannot afford. Other times it is a temptation to eat something our doctor says that we should not eat. Or someone flirted with you, although you are married, and you are tempted to cheat. The devil will always tempt us. Self-indulgence leads to self-destruction.

"Because he himself suffered when he was tempted, He is able to help those who are being tempted."

Hebrews 2:18

Men can learn to resist temptation by thinking of the consequences. It can destroy your marriage and God can send you punishment. The temptation for a drug addict to get one more fix; for an alcoholic, it is to take just one drink.

We are all tempted every day. When we are tempted, understand it is coming from the devil and his forces. Demons roam around everyone, tempting all of us to do wrong. We must listen to God and ignore any wrong thoughts. Remember that temptation is not a sin. Jesus was tempted. We are all tempted, so do not feel guilty being tempted. It is only when we act upon temptation that we sin.

"We have all sinned and fall short of the glory of God."

Romans 3:23

LIVING IN THE "FLESH"

When we become born again, our spirit fills with the "Fruits of the Spirit," and becomes perfect. In addition, we are granted all the power and qualities of Jesus. However, most of us will not transfer all this perfect Spirit to our mind and body. Paul warned that if we continue the sinful nature of this world as it is today, we will continue to resist living and dwelling within our Spirit. We can only succeed with victory over the Devil's lies and temptation if we stop living in the flesh.

When we fail to recognize the dangers and consequences of sin, we allow ourselves to become obsessed with it. We do not even realize that we are in danger of self-destruction, the devil's goal for us. The sins of the flesh are not just carnal sins.

160

"Now, the works of the flesh are evident: sexual immorality, impurity, sensuality, idolatry, sorcery, enmity, strife, jealousy, fits of anger, rivalries, dissensions, divisions, envy, drunkenness, orgies, and things like these. I warn you, as I warned you before, that those who do such things will not inherit the kingdom of God."

Galatians 5:19-2

Whoops! What happened to the words we all heard? The "believe in Jesus and you will be saved," we all have heard in church services? In a perfect world, we could live a perfect life of obedience to the word of God. However, none of us are perfect. We all will continue to make mistakes occasionally.

We cannot be obsessed with any of the sins listed in the scripture above. God will forgive us our current and past mistakes, but we must repent of living in full-time sin. If we do not, we will not make the cut.

"For I tell you that unless your righteousness surpasses that of the Pharisees and the teachers of the law, you will certainly not enter the kingdom of heaven."

Matthew 5:20

Do we live seeking the influence of the Devil, or do we seek guidance from God? That is our choice, and God did give us the freedom of choice. Living within the commandments and rules separates us from unbelievers who live in the flesh. Even if we think we believe in Jesus, we do not know Him if we continue to live in the flesh. In the eyes of God, those that constantly live in the flesh are unbelievers.

Some believe that God does not hear the prayers of unbelievers.

161

"We know that God does not listen to sinners. He listens to the godly man who does his will."

John 9:31

However, God hears everyone; I would think the above would imply that God will ignore the prayers of all those living a full-time life of disobedience. We must be sincere, fully believe and decide to repent. Repentance requires us to change our thinking and our conduct to avoid mistakes. To come out of living in the flesh, we must be saved, by accepting Jesus as our Lord and Savior. In doing so, not only do all our sins become forgiven, but we become "born again" in spirit.

"That which is born of the flesh is flesh, and that which is born of the Spirit is spirit."

John 3:6

We must understand that although we are born again in spirit, our flesh remains flesh. Our body remains in flesh until we die. However, when our body is resurrected, our perfect spirit will join up with our new transfigured perfect body. Our spirit joins up with our new transfigured to a perfect body.

"Sin came through the pride of Lucifer and salvation came through the humility of Jesus."

Zac Poonen

162

THE DEVIL IS A LIAR

Many who do wrong things accept lies from the devil. Anything he tempts us to do should be ignored and avoided. There are two choices of voices in our head that we can choose to listen. They are messages from God or temptations from the devil. We have the *free will* to choose.

However, if we choose the wrong voice and plant a bad seed, it will grow into a fundamental problem for us down the road. This is a seed that will harvest terrible consequences. The devil is a smart liar. He starts with very mild temptations in gray areas. But we become bored, and so, desensitized to the temptations as they grow increasingly serious. Before you know it, we are in a terrible consequential addiction. Therefore, we must choose the right voice to listen to without switching.

"We cannot serve two gods, God and the Devil."

Luke 16:13

The devil tries to make us think that living in sin is fun – and it is at first, until the level of the sins grows so horrendous that one's life becomes a living hell.

"Hey, life is short. Enjoy it," is darn poor advice. The devil will tempt us to put false idols before God and to worship these idols. A demonic curse may have affected not just our parents but also our grandparents and even further back in our genealogy. Pray to God to remove these curses from us. We must take authority over them and demand that they leave our minds and bodies. Heed this warning, whenever we do anything to leave the Devil, he will fight us and tempt us even more. He wants to keep control over us once we let him in.

163

We cannot use the excuse that Flip Wilson used to make us laugh:

"The devil made me do it."

Imagine standing before God on judgment day and trying that one!

The devil is powerless. He can tempt us to do wrong, but our spirit within is much stronger than the devil. He has no power to make us do anything. When we reject the devil and keep God in our hearts, we have the power to shove him away.

"No evil will conquer you; no plague will come near your home."

Psalm 91:10

Beware of the fact that the devil was given two thousand years to bring his wickedness and snarls into our lives. Tribulation is due soon, but no one knows when, regardless of the theories and formulas they try to sell to us. But the day will come when Jesus takes over and the devil will be sent to hell for a thousand years. Then he will return briefly once again to bring temptation back to us but will then be sent to a bottomless pit for eternity.

Chapter 14

TURN TO GOD

ASK GOD FOR HELP

We are never alone; our Lord protects us even in the lonely darkness of the night when our demons reach out to us. God is with us every moment, every day, and we should have faith in His power.

But are we with God every day? Do we really know God, the father, the son, Jesus, and the Holy Spirit?

Going to church every Sunday does not mean that our knowledge of the word of our God is correct and that we have opened a line of communication with Him. We need to know God before we can start asking Him for help.

Think that you need help and ask a stranger for aid. Why would a stranger help us if he does not know us well? Like creating new friendships or mending older ones, we need to work at knowing God. How? We need to listen to a Christian radio station, watch faith movies, go to church, read the bible, join bible discussion groups, and avoid sinful representations of the devil in all forms of media.

In our daily lives and habits, we need to reform our relationship with God in a positive light. These petty things are something that we can do every day.

"No one is so powerful that they never need help."

Matt Jordan

This will bring us close to God to ensure that He will listen to our talks and prayers with Him. Get to know Jesus. Watch movies about him and emulate His conduct in how we live. Know that God loves us; His son, Jesus, died to save us from our sins.

"Be careful for nothing; but in everything by prayer and supplication with thanksgiving, let your requests be made known unto God. And the peace of God, which passes all understanding, shall keep your hearts and minds through Jesus."

Philippians 4:6-7

At times, we all need help. No one is immune from problems. However, there are periods of challenging times that just seem too much. We become overwhelmed and powerless. Our productivity is not only down, but so is our level of consciousness, health, happiness, and success.

When we feel helpless, it is time for us to turn our burdens to God by asking Him for help.

"Come to me, all you who are weary and burdened, and I will give you rest."

Matthew 11:28

We do not have to be troubled by the difficulties that our life presents us with. We do not have to live thinking that we are alone and without faith. Our God will grant us solutions to our problems if we ask for His help. There is a lot that He can do when we feel powerless during tough times.

God can turn hatred into love, anger into calmness, sickness into health, sadness into happiness, calamity into peace, indecisiveness into decisiveness, impatience into patience, rudeness into gentleness, weakness into strength, bitterness into forgiveness, and problems into solvable challenges. We can do all things through Christ, strengthening us when we believe and ask for His help.

It has been said:

"Seven days without God makes one weak."

WHAT IS "BORN AGAIN?"

Christians are advised to become born again in many churches. Questions had risen like, "How can we be born again when we were already born?"

The answer lies within our spirit, not our body. Our body is a fragile shell that can buckle under the pressure of time's passing. Meanwhile, our spirits can be born again when we accept Jesus as our Lord and Savior. Like the light of the sun, our spirit can burn in radiant splendor if we allow the love of our Lord to nourish it.

We become part of the Temple of God. Our spirit becomes all-powerful and perfect. It never has to be saved again. The mind and body may make mistakes, but this does not affect our born-again spirit.

When we are born again, new responsibilities come along with that.

167

"Walk in spirit, and do not fulfill our lust of flesh,"

Galatians 5:16

We must try to live a holy life obeying the commandments and the Golden Rule of our Lord. We must keep in mind that our thoughts turn into actions. Our actions into habits, our habits into our lifestyle, and our lifestyle determines our destination on the Day of Judgement. How we think determines all that follows.

We have the power to determine our destiny if we control each step in the above, and not only that, but the Lord has also created the universe and everything within it. As His servants, we are viceroys of this universe, and we must act according to His command as He is our creator.

"Jesus answered and said to him, "Truly, truly, I say to you, unless one is born again, he cannot see the kingdom of God."

John 3:3

These are some of the new powers our spirit gains when we are born again:

- o Full wisdom
- o Knowledge of everything
- o Full fruits of the spirit
- o Power to perform miracles
- o Power to heal ourselves
- o Power to heal others
- o Full understanding of the truth
- o Power to pray in tongues
- o Complete holiness

Our spirit has the potential to channel the healing powers of Jesus Christ. Though we may not be able to conjure miracles

168

regardless, the little deeds we impart to the world can have a similar impact.

In the next segment, I will explain why these powers are locked away from our minds and bodies.

WHAT HINDERS OUR SPIRIT POWER?

As you recall in the previous chapters, the figures of the triangles depict our inner power in relation to stress levels within our consciousness. I explained why we could not reach the triangle's apex, where we could use the power of Jesus to move the mountains in our lives.

A myriad of external and internal factors is beyond our control, hindering our rise to peak power. Us humans lead a difficult life. From day-to-day habits, we carry responsibilities and outside forces out of our control upon our shoulders. We face too many obstacles and hindrances in life. Just breathing toxins that are in the air and our homes reduces our level of consciousness and our self-control. Like a chalice that cannot hold water, the stress of everyday life overflows from us.

We are bound to *"lose it"* when someone does or says something we hate to hear.

Do not be ashamed when it happens; if you are human, you are bound to make mistakes. Living a perfect life is not humanly possible. No matter how we try to be perfect, it is impossible to do

169

so. Another aspect of this makes it impossible to adhere to the message in Romans 12.2.

"Do not conform to the patterns of this world but be transformed by the renewal of your mind."

Romans 12:2

This scripture is a huge obstacle, like trying to walk through a brick wall. As I wonder why, after being born again, how come, if we have the power of Jesus in the Spirit within, why do we not have this power in our body? We would have to live 100% per Romans 12:2 to achieve our full capabilities, whichever is impossible for us.

Again, we are humans, and it is okay!

Let us look at the importance of Romans 12:2 in the bible. It is the key to why we cannot fully transfer the power of our newborn spirit to our imperfect mind and body.

While our newborn spirit has the power to move mountains, we can understand why God made it impossible for us to reach that level of power. Just think, a terrorist could think and knock a building down without doing anything to make it happen.

Picture this. The box on our left represents our new perfect spirit within that has all the power of Jesus. But here is the problem. We can only do so much to transfer this power to our mind and body because Romans 12:2 is tough to get through.

170

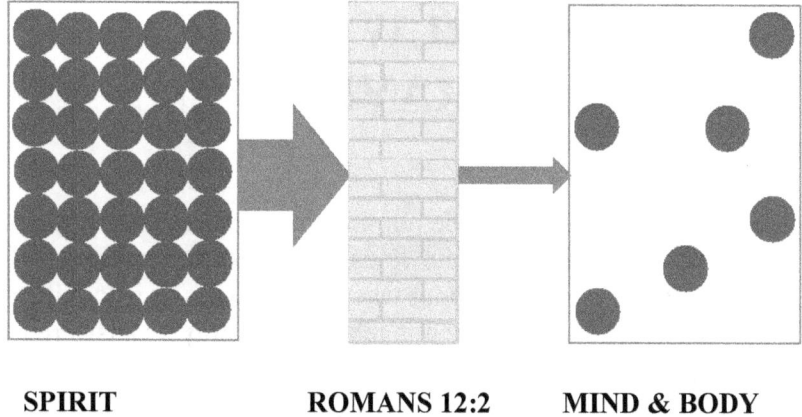

SPIRIT   **ROMANS 12:2**   **MIND & BODY**

As you see in the drawing, the circles in our Spirit represent untapped power that sits latent. To trigger the metamorphosis of our body and mind, we must find the catalyst to achieve a perfect mental and physical state.

But what is the obstacle that barres us from achieving this state? As you can see from the diagram, the wall that sits between our goal is Romans 12:2. Represented by the circles, it needs to diffuse through the wall of understanding Romans 12:2 to nourish our mind and body, and the amount differs for each of us, as we differ in obedience.

It is like trying to get through a brick wall. Hopefully, this pictorially helps you to understand why our mind and body will never have the power to move mountains.

171

DOES GOD ALWAYS HEAR OUR PRAYERS?

We depend on and place our faith in tangible things throughout our life. Many times, in our lives, we question the power of the Lord. We ask questions about whether He exists or is looking over us. Many feel that they are not getting their prayers answered, and this lack of faith is why we live a life of sin 24/7.

How long can we stay within the haze of drugs, alcohol, lies, or whatever wrongful duties we indulge in? Scripture says that God will not listen to the prayers of anyone who lives full-time in sin.

It is right in the bible for all to see.

"We know that God does not listen to sinners. He listens to the godly person who does his will."

John 9:31

I do not take this literally.

God hears all prayers and forgives all but is aware of our deeds. Think of him as a father; should a father reward the behavior of children who continue to disobey him and run down a road that leads to their oblivion? Though He loves all of us, He wants to teach us a lesson. Hence, He ignores answering prayers from anyone living 24/7 in sin.

For a sinner who turns to God, do not fear that He will never hear your prayers. He loves all of us very much, and He will forgive us and listen to our prayers. In exchange for His love, we are told to repent and not violate God's commandments. To avoid bad conduct, we must think and do things that are pure, noble, just, and righteous most of the time.

Most of the time, if we try to live a righteous life, God hears our prayers. He loves those who listen to His words and are kind to the world in turn. Like any fatherly figure, they talk about their children or grandchildren as being the "apple of our eye."

Well, to God, we are the "apple of His eye."

"For this is what the Lord Almighty says: "After the Glorious One has sent me against the nations that have plundered you, for whoever touches you, touches the apple of His eye"

Zechariah 2:8

God does answer our prayers according to His timing, not our timing. He must consider all those praying, not just ours. Also, remember that sometimes, not getting an answer is His way of saying, no, as the prayer may not be in your or someone else's best interest. God knows that.

When you pray, always say, "Let Thy will and not my will, be done."

One word of caution that we often overlook is never to try to negotiate with God. We should not pray for something and offer God a bargain deal, for example, "Please, God, let me win the lottery, and I swear I'll give my church a million dollars."

"...the great God, mighty and awesome, who shows not partiality and accepts no bribes."

Deuteronomy 10-17

173

JESUS MADE BIBLE CORRECTIONS

Jesus clarified the marked differences in the Old Testament. He did not want us to take revenge on those who harmed us, and some scriptures were far too complex for the followers to understand. Therefore, Jesus aided us.

"You have heard that it was said, 'Eye for eye, and a tooth for a tooth.' But I tell you, do not resist an evil person. If anyone slaps you on the right cheek, turn to them the other cheek also."

Matthew 5:38

Also, Jesus did not want us to hate our enemies.

"You have heard that it was said, 'Love your neighbor and hate your enemy.' But I tell you, love your enemies and pray for those who persecute you that you may be children of your Father in heaven. He causes the sun to rise and the evil and the good and sends rain on the righteous and the unrighteous."

Matthew 5:43

There are times we feel that we hate our enemies and may even wish them dead, but this is not what Lord commands. We must send peace, light, and love to those who attack us. We must believe that vengeance is God's.

"If your enemy is hungry, give him food to eat, and if he is thirsty, give him water to drink. In doing this, you will heap burning coals on his head, and the LORD will reward you."

Proverbs 25:22

MORNING PRAYER

A particularly important part of avoiding tough times is to start each day with a positive routine. To avoid waking up from the *wrong side* of the bed, we need to believe that there is no wrong side.

We sleep on a comfortable bed with sheets barring us from the cold. Some people in the world do not even have this simple luxury. If you view life in such a light, you will thank the Lord for every blessing.

As soon as we wake up, we should thank God for another day of life and the food he blesses on our table. Then we must start our morning prayers based on scripture; this prayer helps me set the tone of how I would like my day to go.

"This is the day the Lord has made; I will rejoice and be glad in it."

Psalm 118:24

"I will not let my heart be troubled."

John 14:1

"I can do all things through Christ who strengthens me."

Philippians 4:13

Memorize these without the scripture names and numbers. Create a prayer like this, asking God for help.

175

"God, I cannot live like this anymore, and I cannot continue to try to do this alone. I need you. I need to change how I am living in my life. I have been doing it all wrong, thinking I was in control and could do it all alone. But I cannot. Please help me, Lord. I am placing my life on the cross of Jesus and pray you will guide my path out of this hell I am living in. Lord, let your will and not my will be done."

Use your own words to thank God and to pray for your needs. Follow your morning prayers by creating and using some positive affirmations like:

"I choose to be happy, healthy, successful, harmonious, calm, energetic, and positive in my outlook. Whenever I feel worried, I will turn my attention to God and turn my worries into faith, knowing He loves me."

"I will not let myself be offended by anyone."

"I place myself, my loved ones, my problems, and my decisions in the Lord's hands."

GET RID OF PRIDE

We must resist the temptation to "wave our own flag." Pride within our mortal bodies will get us nowhere. In moderation, it is healthy to believe in oneself regardless; excess pride rots one's spirit. We must always work hard for the glory of God and let others praise our works if deserved.

Excessive pride in oneself ignores the fact that we cannot live a fully healthy, happy, and successful life. It implies that we can do anything without God. We all need God, and we all need the help of others. We must live within the glory of the Lord when we decide to stop living in the flesh.

God expelled Lucifer from heaven due to his excessive pride. That is how much the Lord hates pride and egotism; when we expel expressive pride within ourselves, we invite the devil into our hearts.

Others will sense that and not like us very much, and we are also repelling God and violating His teachings. It is far better to focus on God than on us. Pray for God to lead your way.

".... let Your will and not my will be done."

Matthew 26:39

Rather than continuing to live in the flesh with an 'I can do it all!' attitude, one should remain humble, albeit hopeful that his fate will change. We should pray daily for God to lead our way, letting His will and not our will be done.

In short, we stop being selfish and turn pride, egotism and conceit into humbleness and humility as we bow before the Lord and ask Him to lead our way.

177

Chapter 15

CHANGE OUR LIFE

CHANGE YOUR LIFE

"Better keep yourself clean and bright. You are the window through which you must see the world."

George Bernard Shaw

To change oneself for the betterment of society and the afterlife, one must acknowledge their faults and be ready for change. If we feel we need to change our life, we must start by changing our thoughts.

Make a list of all that you want. We should get a photo of each thing that we want to earn and purchase. Place the photos on your wall and keep picturing yourself having them. If you work hard and have faith, you will have the things you desire.

If what we are doing is not working for us, it is time to change what we are doing. If our life is a continuous stream of demanding times, we need to take the steps suggested in the book

If we are doing things that lead to problem after problem, with no breaks, it is time to stop and define mistakes that we are making that bring on tough times. We should ask, am I doing what God created me to do? Then analyze whether your daily activity, job or whatever you do is right or wrong.

And if you cannot decide that, go to get counseling. If you cannot afford it, go to a church, and find a pastor with whom you can be honest and have a heart-to-heart.

Tell the pastor honestly what you are doing. If it is wrong, you certainly are not doing what God created you to do. If we repeat mistakes or hate our jobs, we will always be unsatisfied with our lives and unhappy and depressed. When our minds are stuck in the eye of a storm, we cannot think or function clearly; hence it leaves us to wonder, what is wrong with me?

The past is the past, and it is gone. We must not wallow in our past mistakes; instead, we learn from them and create a better future.

"Rid yourselves of all the offenses you have committed and get a new heart and a new spirit."

Ezekiel 18:31

We need to change if we have been leading a full-time life of doing wrong things and making bad decisions. Time is precious; if we do not take control of ourselves, we lose most of it. If we do not, troubled times will surely continue to haunt us. We must change how we think and what we do, even if it means sacrificing some activities we might love most.

It is difficult, but the consequence of it will refresh your lifestyle. There can be no more lust, alcohol, narcotics, prostitution, greed, gossip, and crime. Once we decide to throw away these soulless activities from our lives, we will break the shackles of sin, for this is to worship false idols.

179

"If a righteous person turns from their righteousness and commits sin, they will die for it; but if a wicked person turns away from the wickedness and does what is just and right, they will save their life."

Ezekiel 18:26-27

Paul said that when we are saved, our being becomes the temple of God. Think of the advantage that we Christians have; it is like we each have our own God who hears our prayers. He does more than that, according to scripture. He is interceding which means that he prays for us. You should pray for God's will, not your will, to be done.

Knowledge is power. If you read the Bible with your heart and mind, you will understand that the truth sets you free from worldly shackles.

"If you do not know the truth, it is killing you."

Andrew Wommack

The truth is in the Bible, and it is a good idea to read it regularly with a regular schedule. In addition, if you are not in a bible-based church, you need to go church-shopping to visit some Christian churches. Remember, the building is not for which you are shopping. The church is the minister, staff, and all the members.

As we visit a church service, we must pay attention and think about what is being preached and distance ourselves from worldly matters like building castles in Spain and daydreaming of luxuries. We should observe the people in worship... if they are full in the Spirit, they will have smiles on their faces. That is when the Spirit of God is felt.

While abundance is ours to take, how we earn it determines our reputation with the people around us and our Lord. People judge us by our deeds and our words. If we are doing the sad things above, everybody knows it. We can improve and change our reputation when we stop and clean up our act.

"If we keep eternity in mind, we can make better decisions on how we think and act!"

Matt Jordan

ENJOY LIFE

"There are only two ways to live your life; One is as though nothing is a miracle; the other is as though everything is a miracle."

Albert Einstein

To create a radiant future, we must keep in mind that there is nothing we can do to change the past, but we can learn from it. Like a babe who learns as it grows, human civilization has done the same as it evolves. Every slight change we make is enough to impact our future.

It is fascinating to think that all the souls in this world can make a collective change. Visualize a tiny firefly. On its own, it cannot create much light, but a sparkle of them can light vast areas. We need to enjoy being alive, embrace the person God created us to be, and practice true righteousness and holiness.

Life is precious.

We need to stop making "mountains out of molehills" and deal with our problems with patience. Take one step at a time, prioritize

181

your time, and be kind to those passing you by. Greet everyone with a smile on your face. When you bring joy to others and make them feel good, you feel better yourself and people enjoy being around you, even if it is just a person at a cash register.

Treat others as you want to be treated, then watch your mood shift.

A fulfilled life is a blessing that is rewarded when we change our hearts and are reborn with Christ's power. Whatever we do, do it the best you can, understanding that we are doing God's work and doing it for the glory of God.

Hard times will continue to come to us, but we should use the solutions in this book to rise victorious and work towards our goals and future.

"The future belongs to those who believe in the beauty of their dreams."

Eleanor Roosevelt.

Now let us bring the light of righteousness into our lives and into the lives of others.

THE TEN COMMANDMENTS

1. YOU SHALL HAVE NO OTHER IDOLS OR GODS BEFORE ME

This world is colorful and diverse. Each region in the world has its own culture, therefore, religion. Some say, "I kind of follow the principle laid out by Buddha."

Be tolerant towards those who have always been from a different religion, but if you are a Christian, do not stray away from your teachings. If we want to be Christians, we cannot violate the first commandment. Remember, Judeo-Christian churches require loyalty to the ten commandments.

2. THOU SHALL NOT TAKE THE LORD'S NAME IN VAIN

Who among us has not sworn when something quickly angers us? As humans, we are prone to anger and other highly emotional stimuli, but we must work to avoid this. How? Channel this energy into creativity rather than allowing your anger spell to control you like *confound it*, silly?

But try something.

183

3. REMEMBER THE SABBATH DAY AND KEEP IT HOLY

As we all know, Christians have chosen Sunday as their holy day, but Jews believe it is Saturday.

Not too long ago, many Christian churches began having Saturday services so that we could choose which day to pick. Whatever you choose your Sabbath day to be, Jesus said we should worship and rest on that day.

4. HONOR YOUR FATHER AND MOTHER

Honor means to love, obey, and respect them. God wanted peace in the home. He did not want children talking back and rebelling against their parents, so He made this law.

5. THOU SHALL NOT KILL

God wanted us to protect others and not kill them. However, we all know that the police and military must occasionally kill to protect others. When one becomes a guardian, there are times when one needs to hold a sword to the throat of the enemy.

Ironic, but necessary.

6. THOU SHALL NOT COMMIT ADULTERY

Lust lies within the heart of all men and women, it is as natural as the wind that flows on this Earth. Relishing this emotion is where many make a mistake. Many men felt or feel that having sex outside of marriage for fun is not wrong. God requires the husband and the wife to be faithful and not commit adultery.

7. THOU SHALL NOT STEAL

This is not just God's law but the law of any sophisticated society. Looting in times of riots has been a huge problem in this country. We cannot take something that belongs to others, not just from a store, but even from our homes.

8. THOU SHALL NOT LIE OR BEAR FALSE WITNESS

We cannot lie about anything, expressing anything other than the truth. The truth hurts sometimes, but in the end, it is the best thing to comply with to avoid hurting others or even yourself.

9. THOU SHALL NOT COVET THY NEIGHBOR'S WIFE

We are not supposed to admire and envy someone else's spouse.

10. THOU SHALL NOT COVET THY NEIGHBOR'S GOODS

We should not try to "keep up with the Joneses" nor wish we had anything that belongs to them, whether a pool, new car, boat, or whatever. Be thankful for what you have and pray for abundance for others.

Finally, I believe that obeying the "Golden Rule" covers most of the other laws of God in the bible. I define it this way:

"Do not do or say unto others what you would not want them to do or say unto you."

185

I am sure some of you readers out there are asking, "What does understanding and obeying God's laws have to do with this book?"

We need to learn that our thoughts and conduct are causing many of the trials we face today by violating the laws. This part of the book aims to understand what we can do to avoid tough times.

REVIEW OF OUR CONDUCT

It would not be a bad idea for us to review our level of obedience to God's rules. We must be honest with ourselves as God knows whether we are or not.

GOLDEN RULE

- Do we listen to our children, parents, and others before we snap at them?
- Do we give others notice when we are running late?
- Do we yell at others when they get us angry?
- Do we take vengeance when offended by others?
- Do we take time to help our relatives and friends through a challenging time?

FRUITS OF SPIRIT

- Do we take time to tell our loved ones that we love them?
- Do we avoid loud arguments in our homes?
- Are we patient with interruptions, criticism, long lines, traffic lights, and others?
- Are we kind to everyone in our manner?
- Do we try to be good citizens in our community?
- Are we faithful to God, our spouse, church, and our friends?
- Are we gentle in trying to teach or correct others?
- Do we exercise self-control when someone tells us how bad they think we are?

TEN COMMANDMENTS

- Do we spend too much time with false idols, like cell phones, television, and movie stars?
- Do we far too often take the Lord's name in vain?
- Do we honor our father and mother, both in life and death?
- Do we cheat on our spouse?
- Do we steal from others?
- Do we lie, including "white lies?"
- Do we wish we had our neighbor's goods?

This was a tough lesson but a necessary one. I know that following these rules will be tough for each of you but let us work on it together!

"Actions bring consequences, or they can bring rewards. Is it not wonderful that we have a choice?"

Matt Jordan

Chapter 16

WHEN KNOCKED DOWN

GET BACK UP

The sea that we call Life is unpredictable, and our voyage upon it is filled with difficulties. We all are knocked down many times in life.

We lose a loved one that we feel we cannot live without. Or we lost our job or went bankrupt, or whatever. Sometimes, we all get into something so bad that we feel life is over for us. We lose our desire to live, thinking life will never be the same.

Just understand that the devil wants us to stay down. If we lose a close loved one, a spouse, parents, sibling, or child. We have a right to cry, mourn, feel depressed and be sad. Acknowledging and acting upon our grief is important for us to find peace afterward.

If we lose a job or face monetary loss, we must get right back up and get on with our life. No matter what each period of challenging times is about, we must remember that we have not yet reached our destiny. Our destiny will always be in a state of ebb and flow. We must analyze our obstacles and find alternatives so that we never stay stagnant.

If we fail to plan, we plan to fail. Set new goals. Get back up and get busy with getting on with your life. Go after your new goals with perseverance and additional focus, and remember that God is with you.

"Obstacles are what we see when we lose sight of our goals. Stay focused in a laser, straight ahead direction towards achieving our goals. Conquer the obstacles and forge ahead for the prize."

Matt Jordan

We must conduct our purpose in life. Happiness, health, and success can be ours if we prioritize our time and goals. Life goes fast. Time moves on and does not wait for us to lay on the couch and wallow in our tough times.

Time is nothing for God; thousand years pass for him simultaneously for us to take a single breath of air.

"'For I know the plans I have for you,' declares the Lord, 'Plans to prosper you and not to harm you, plans to give you hope and a future.'"

Jeremiah 29:11

GAIN WISDOM

A great idea to help us conquer challenging times is to gain the power of wisdom. Not everyone has wisdom because they have not experienced life to its full extent yet. We have all dealt with intelligent people that lack common sense and wisdom.

190

Many do not even know what wisdom is, it took me many years to develop it, and I become wiser each year. Wisdom comes from gaining a lot of experience in life as we gain knowledge and good judgment. It takes time and usually is found in older people, especially seniors. As one gains wisdom, one gains many qualities, for example, understanding of the world, insight, perception, common sense, astuteness, good judgment, foresight, prudence, logic, and soundness.

Wise people can make better decisions, acting with the use of all these qualities of wisdom in time. We make many bad decisions and mistakes, gathering such experiences in our arsenal. We gain the ability to use these quantities over time going through life. Scripture advises us to ask God for wisdom.

"But the wisdom that comes from heaven is first of all pure: then peace-loving, considerate, submissive, full of mercy and good fruit, impartial and sincere."

James 3:17

It's wise for children to work on gaining wisdom by talking to seniors about life, problems, goals, or whatever.

CONTINUE TO GROW

We should never feel immense pride in our abilities and that we have reached the top. Thinking that one has no room to grow is wrong. One of my passions is playing the trumpet. I played operas at just twelve years old. I played first chair trumpet in concert bands all through school and for several years after college. But I never thought I was great, and there was no room to grow.

191

Instead, for many years, my goal has been this; I want to play better than last year. This requires me to continue to practice. When a musician stops practicing and thinks he is great, then on the day of the performance, it will result in a continuous drop in ability.

Sinatra said, "Use it or lose it." This applies to everyone, regardless of our mission in life. Take continuing education classes and learn new things, always trying to improve. Complacency is not a characteristic we should ever want to develop, or we start to go downhill.

"Any man's life will be filled with constant and unexpected encouragement if he makes up his mind to do his level best each day."

Booker T. Washington

CREATE SUCCESS

As we get back up on our feet, we need to set new goals to work on. We discussed how to decide on the work we were born to do and that if we do it, we will not only enjoy the work but also find success.

"Success is to have laughed often and much; to win the respect of intelligent people and affection of children, to earn the appreciation of honest critics and endure the betrayal of false friends; to appreciate beauty, to find the best in others; to leave the world a bit better, whether by a healthy child, a garden patch or a redeemed social condition, to know even one life has breathed easier because you have lived. This is to have succeeded."

Ralph Waldo Emerson

We all should be in a job or business that we love and that fills our day with joy. We can never find success in doing work that we hate. I cover all you need to know on how to succeed in my first book, reviewed in the introduction. Just know success only comes from a lot of sweat, blood, and tears. We must work hard at it full-time.

"But remember the Lord your God, for it is he who gives you the ability to produce wealth, and so confirms his covenant, which he swore to your ancestors, as it is today."

Deuteronomy 8:18

193

LIVE IN PEACE

R.I.P. Rest in peace.

We see this symbol of rest in peace all the time on social media after someone dies. It is a local celebrity, musician, sports star, or someone respected in the community.

Why do we not think, L.I.P., "live in peace?"

Why do we have to get angry when someone offends us? Why can we not brush it off or patiently discuss the situation and compromise? We do not and should not make every disagreement with anyone a war. Both parties of war get hurt, and often others get hurt as well.

We need to decide whether we want to live in peace or live in hell. When we live in peace, others want to be near us. We act calm, and they feel calm. If we act angry, they feel uncomfortable. Imagine yourself standing in front of a mirror; whatever emotion you show will reflect onto the surface. Therein, do we not want to be with people who make us laugh, feel good, and seem peaceful?

Would it not be great if everyone lived peacefully and allowed harmony to take root in our hearts? Living in an angry world will undoubtedly bring us unnecessary wars and trials. Though disagreement and war are in our nature, we do not have to settle arguments through anger. Live in Peace, my readers.

Chapter 17

MAKE POSITIVE

CHANGES

STAY 39 YEARS OLD, 61 MORE TIMES!

Time, age, and wisdom are directly proportional to each other. As time passes, we grow old, make memories, therefore, grow wise.

But when do we become old exactly? Many think they are old at fifty. Guess what? If we think we are old, our bodies will get old. The human brain is a wonderful organ! Our thoughts and perception of the world can significantly impact our bodies.

We will *feel* old if we think we need a cane or a wheelchair if we reach fifty. My dear readers have faith in your body and spirit, do not actively plan to retire from work at sixty-five.

If you retire from a job, then start working on things you love to do that you never had a chance to do. Do the right things to stay healthy and strong. You can make it to one hundred with a good, cheerful outlook and a good sense of humor! Many positive-thinking people do.

"You do not stop laughing when you grow old; you grow old when you stop laughing."

George Bernard Shaw

Age is more than a number; it is an attitude and a choice of lifestyle.

Remember, the mind is all-powerful. Whatever and however we think will influence our lives and physically manifest on our bodies. If you read the bible, many people lived for over one hundred and twenty years!

Moses lived for one hundred and twenty years. Some say he lived for two hundred years. Of course, life was different back then when a healthy lifestyle was normal for them. They had to walk a lot because they did not have cars. They had to work harder, lacking the inventions that made our life easier. They did not have food loaded with pesticides and chemical preservatives. The air did not have hundreds of toxins due to zero control over industrial emissions, especially in China.

In my first book, I explained how I loved a positive idea from Jack Benny. He coined the phrase, "I'm thirty-nine!"

When I reached thirty-nine, I decided to stay thirty-nine in attitude and keep myself busy through work along with other healthy extracurricular activities.

I would never retire. My family knew I was older, but I was always treated as thirty-nine. This trend was incorporated into my daily lifestyle to the point where they gave 39-year-old birthday cards.

196

When I climbed over thirty-nine, I continued to go to the gym, and work, and I still work long days as a senior. I write, play music, write music, invest in real estate, and keep busy all day long. I take supplements to release toxins and replace the lost vitamins from food. My wife and I go for long walks frequently.

To avoid unnecessary troubled times, we must stay active to stay young and healthy and enjoy life to the fullest. Never retire to a rocking chair or become a "couch potato."

Jesus said:

"If you can believe, all things are possible to him who believes."

Mark 9:23

THE MANY DANGERS OF SMOKING

This will not only help you to avoid challenging times, but this segment may save your life!

I can hear you smokers now, "Why does he have to bug me on this? I get this all the time."

The reason is this. Most think, well, smoking causes cancer. I have a good chance that I won't because my aunt smoked until she was ninety. Well, your aunt was just lucky. There are many dangers of smoking, and we all need to know what they are.

I spent a lot of time researching this because I had a nephew dying of lung cancer from smoking. Unfortunately, he held on too

197

long, and it was far too late to stop his passing at a far too young age. Watching him drop under one hundred pounds and seeing him suffer was extremely hard for all of us family members.

Smoking causes many diseases, destroys our health, and harms most of the organs in our body, causing grief within the hearts of our loved ones.

Stopping in time will save your life. Every year, there are almost 500,000, one-third of our deaths in our country. Many do not know that more than ten times as many of our citizens have died too young, more than all our war deaths combined! It causes more than just lung cancer.

The following is a list of problems that active and passive smoking can cause:

1. BLOCKAGE OF BLOOD TO THE LEGS

Smoking can cause a blockage of our blood flow to the legs causing severe pain and walking problems.

2. CORONARY HEART DISEASE

Many do not know that smoking can obstruct arteries and cause massive heart attacks. My sister died at the incredibly early age of fifty-one of a heart attack that I believe was caused by her heavy smoking of cigarettes.

3. STROKE AND BLOOD PRESSURE

A stroke happens when a blood clot causes a blockage of blood flow to the brain. A vessel in or around our brain bursts.

Smoke causes blood vessels to get thick and get narrow. This makes the heartbeat faster and, of course, high blood pressure.

4. COPD (Chronic Obstructive Pulmonary Disease)

I stopped smoking years ago but caught this playing in bars loaded with smoke. Many have this disease and still smoke, which I seriously do not understand.

5. EMPHYSEMA

Emphysema is a lung condition that causes shortness of breath. Most of us have seen people with this disease coughing while smoking cigarettes. Is that crazy or what? I am sorry but seeing people killing themselves due to nicotine addiction bothers me.

Yes, smoking is another addiction.

OTHER AFFECTED AREAS:

- Cervix
- Pancreas
- Colon
- Liver
- Esophagus
- Teeth and Gums
- Stomach
- Pregnancy
- Cataracts
- Kidneys

- Larynx

- Inflammation and Arthritis

- Type 2 Diabetes Mellitus

So, we can see that there are many different and life-threatening problems, yet we catch just one. One is enough to kill us.

Anyone who knows all the information in this segment yet does not stop smoking is committing slow and painful suicide. The chance of surviving it is based upon how quickly we catch the symptoms.

UNDERSTANDING "FREE WILL"

We all have heard that God gave us "Free Will." What does that mean? Can we make choices that will determine our destiny? God gave us the ability to choose between right and wrong decisions. These choices can result in good or bad outcomes. Scripture gives us the good news of free will, but all must recognize the consequence of making the wrong choices.

However, free will does not give us the freedom to violate scripture rules. The ramifications of wrong choices should make us think better about how we use our freedom of choice. Does this freedom tempt us to do what is wrong?

When we use "free will," it should be to decide whether to take a rightful or wrongful direction on a decision we make.

"I have the right to do anything, you say—but not everything is beneficial. I have the right to do anything—but not everything is constructive."

1 Corinthians 10:23

We ought to know whether an action we are thinking of taking is right or wrong in the eyes of God. Wrong choices will have consequences that will lead to tough times.

"...Free will does not mean one will, but many wills conflicting in one man. Freedom cannot be conceived simply."

Flannery O'Connor

DAILY TIME MANAGEMENT

This may be the most important segment in this book. Failure to practice time management will cause health problems and lead to divorce, addictions, anger issues, fear, worry, excess stress, insomnia, sleep deprivation, and many more demanding times.

Many of us have too many things on our to-do list.

"There are numerous things that we all would like or need to do each day, but the truth is, we cannot do them all."

Matt Jordan

We often create our own anxiety. We all are going through incredibly stressful times, seeing and interacting with incredibly stressed people wherever we go. Stress is like wildfire; once the fire starts, it is hard to control it.

201

Most of us make the first mistake of putting a lot of pressure on our shoulders. This requires us to rush from task to task and even sometimes run from place to place. We create a work speed that creates stress and causes anxiety, which leads to "panic attacks" in many people because they cannot bear the pressure anymore.

Stress often leads to insomnia, sleep deprivation, illness and even death. We must avoid all this to create a work pace that does not require us to rush. We need to plan only the things we can do at a calm pace.

Each morning, after you finish my suggested morning routine, it is time to write down everything you need or want to do. Cross off the things you did and add new tasks progressively. Prioritize your list and move some items out into a one-week plan. We cannot accomplish this with just a daily plan. Both women and men are faced with stressful lives, trying to do too much.

Whoever normally does the one-week grocery shopping cannot expect to do this during the week at 4:45 PM, and get all that done, go home, cook, and do all of that without getting stressed. You would put that on your weekend schedule, and if you stop in a store on your way home during the week, it would be just for a few things you run out of, like milk, bread, and eggs. Spouses should share in the short stops to the grocery during the week.

During our work week, we need a time plan.

Remember, sleep does not remove stress. If you go to bed with a stressed mind, the likelihood of waking up in a similar state is high. We cannot skip a morning routine. Meditation requires at least twenty minutes alone. The more days we skip this, the further down our level of consciousness will drop, losing our strength and power levels.

During our work week, we need a time plan.

6 - 7 AM is a wonderful time to meditate, pray, read some Bible, and do breathing exercises.

7 - 8 AM is the time to revise the "things to do" list. For example, I do some stretching and use light weights for some exercise. I read and answer emails or messages on my cell phone, shower, and leave for the office.

8 AM - 5 PM, a work period with a break in the middle. After dinner, it is nice to spend time reading, working on a hobby, practicing music if we play, talking to someone, playing a game, watching shows on the TV, or other activities that calm me down.

"Lack of direction, not lack of time, is the problem. We all have twenty-four-hour days."

Zig Ziglar

TAKE TIME TO RELAX

We are all stressed from the life we have all been thrown into. We all have too much to do. We work hard and find ourselves very tired; we are upset with inflation, rude drivers blowing their horns at us, long lines, or horrific news. However, we must take some time every day to just relax.

Try reading an informative book that captures you on page one – one you just *cannot* put down. We all did a lot of that in the past, but in our chaotic new lives, we left reading out of our schedules. But a delightful book, with a little soft background music, like classical piano, is a wonderful way to unwind. We also stop thinking about troublesome topics when reading a book or watching a great movie.

203

If you have Netflix, Amazon Prime, or some other source of movies, try to search for "faith-based movies," as they are not only relaxing, but inspirational. There are a lot of garbage movies out there designed to poison the youth and pull adults towards accepting anything that can be considered bad conduct.

Take time to pray and meditate to remove stress and to rise in the level of consciousness. Set a time each day for your relaxation period, and since we all have different schedules and work times, it could be in the morning, afternoon, or evening. Just try to make it at least half an hour.

It is also great to go to a favorite place outside to relax, if possible.

"Come away by yourselves to a desolate place and rest a while."

Mark 6:31

WE CAN STILL HAVE FUN

God advises us that if we live holy lives, good things happen. We can still have fun without drugs or alcohol. When we get off all addictions, we find out:

"Sober is the new high,"

Matt Jordan

When we live a holy life of obedience, we avoid many problems and subsequently enjoy a happier life. Also, we become better respected by all we encounter. Respect is not coming to us automatically because of our status, job, or popularity. Our conduct in front of others must earn respect. We become more trusted, liked, and people should enjoy being around us.

We can still joke around and make people laugh. I like to make people laugh. I find just creating funny comments around the conversation that is going on makes people laugh.

We cannot live a holy life while continuing to swear, tell filthy jokes, commit adultery, steal, lie or disobey God's laws.

Chapter 18

UNDERSTANDING

REVELATION

DESCRIBING REVELATION

We cannot change the bible's predictions in revelation and cannot do anything to prevent it. However, I believe we can slow down the start date of Tribulation if we do the right things. God revealed to John at the Island of Pathos what would happen during the revelation. The earth is going to suffer severe plagues, including intense heat, drought, hailstones, apocalypse, tornadoes, and locusts destroying all in their paths. Water will turn to blood. Humankind will also suffer from lice, gnats, diseased livestock, boils, and hail. There will be three days of darkness. As the storms begin, the stars and planets will turn into scary shapes like dinosaurs.

"Then the temple of God was opened in heaven, and the ark of His covenant was seen in His temple. And there was lightning, noises, thundering, an earthquake, and great hail."

Revelation 11:19

206

Some of the disasters are already occurring but will get much worse during the tribulation.

"Nation will rise against nation, and kingdom against kingdom. There will be earthquakes in various places and famines and troubles. These are the beginning of sorrows."

Mark 13:8

It is majestic to watch and listen to a huge storm – the magnitude of lightning and rumbling thunder reminds us of God's unlimited power of God, who created everyone everywhere. God's majesty will be proclaimed throughout the entire universe. His voice will thunder throughout the heavens. The lightning also will reveal God's unlimited power and sovereignty over all creation. The thunder will accompany the most potent storm we have ever experienced. We will lose our light from the sun.

"The sun shall be no more thy light by day, neither for brightness shall the moon give light unto thee: but the Lord shall be unto thee an everlasting light, and the God thy glory."

Isaiah 60:19

The good news is that Christians believe that we will be raptured, taken up into the sky, and spared the worst part of the seven years of tribulation. Knowing this, we must be ready, which requires us to repent in order to be among those raptured.

Jesus said that no one knows when this will happen despite many Ministers trying to predict the start date. No one means no one, including priests, reverends, and any ministers of the word. The new Jerusalem will come down from the sky to house Christians.

"He carried me away in the Spirit to a great and high mountain and showed me the great city, the holy Jerusalem, descending out of heaven from God, having the glory of God. Her light was like a most precious stone, like a jasper stone, clear as crystal."

Revelation 21:9-11

There is an ongoing debate on when the rapture will occur before, in the middle, or at the end of Tribulation. I believe it will be before the sad things start to happen.

WHAT OUR SPIRIT TAKES TO HEAVEN

What are the things in life we can take into Heaven? We cannot take our house, cash, gold, silver, stock accounts, massive television, stereo set, or anything else. So why do we focus on gathering material "stuff?" Would it not make more sense to accumulate enjoyable memories that we can take to heaven and enjoy for eternity?

"The things which we see are temporary, but the things which are not seen are eternal."

2 Corinthians 4:18

We can take all the great memories that we can accumulate. There is no limit; we should take more time to spend with those we love and our walks looking at beautiful nature. We will take the memories of visits to relatives and friends we love. We can take memories of the vacations, games we play, the hobbies we love,

208

and the joy we give others. We can take memories of the trips we take our children on, the days at the park, and time with parents, grandparents, and relatives.

It is time to start allocating more time to accumulating memories.

"Why do we spend so much time accumulating things and so little time accumulating memories?"

Matt Jordan

THIS IS NOT HEAVEN

Many of us spend too much time complaining about the problems we face. We are sick too often. We have too much to do. We feel rushed all day and are too busy. We catch too many red lights. People cut us off on the roads and steal parking spots that we might be heading toward. We feel tired all the time and complain about our age. We have too many problems; people drive us crazy, prices are too high, and we do not have enough money.

This is not heaven. Life will never be easy here on earth. Everything is not going to go smoothly. We do not live in a perfect place – inevitably, things will continue to go wrong.

However, when challenging times come, this book will hopefully help all readers understand the causes of tough times and how to avoid them. If we do, we can reduce the number of challenging times we must fight to get through. Plus, when we do get unexpected, challenging times, this book will better prepare us to remain calm as we do what we must do to solve them calmly and promptly.

The good news is that all these problems we experience will not occur in Heaven.

"For where your treasure is, there your heart will be also."
Matthew 6:21

So, what will heaven be like?

WHAT WILL HEAVEN BE LIKE

Some people claimed to have died, seen heaven and refused to return to life on earth. What they all had in common was to say that it was an amazing, beautiful place that gave them the greatest feelings they had ever felt.

The Bible gave great descriptions of heaven, so I will use more scripture in this section. The first description is of the new Jerusalem that will come down from the sky for all who Christians are saved.

The height, length, and width of New Jerusalem are of equal dimensions. They measure 12,000 furlongs high, wide and in length; that is about 1500 miles for each dimension. That is massive and must be since it will be full of mansions.

Did you ever dream of living in a mansion?

"In My Father's house are many mansions; if it were not so, I would have told you. I am going to prepare a place for you. And if I go and prepare a place for you, I will come again and receive you to Myself; that where I am, there you may be also."

John 14:2-3

There is something that will be multiple times more dazzling than the spectacular mansions in Heaven. The idea of dwelling with Jesus will be the most wonderful experience. We will see His face, and His name will be on our foreheads. As God welcomes us into heaven, the Truth will be the conclusion of our hope in Jesus. In addition, we can take pleasure in knowing that we will all have new, perfect bodies that will not feel pain or suffering. We will assemble with the company of angels and our most holy God.

There will be no more searching for cures for diseases known to man. God will heal every ailment that each of us has with the leaves of the tree. Also, He will fill the fruit of the tree that is in the center of heaven's jeweled street with an overabundance of amazing light.

"They shall see His face, and His name shall be on their foreheads. There shall be no night there: They need no lamp nor light of the sun, for the Lord God gives them light. And they shall reign forever and ever."

Revelation 22:4-5

There will be no problems, but we will not sit on clouds, play the harp, and sing hymns all day. We will be quite busy perusing Heaven, for it is a place of peace, love, and incommunicable beauty with flowers, plants, and nature.

211

"The middle of its street, and on either side of the river, was the tree of life, which bore twelve fruits, each tree yielding its fruit every month. The leaves of the tree were for the healing of the nations."

Revelation 22:2

In our world, strained with sickness and disease, the description above is a beautiful reminder that there will be no more suffering or pain in heaven. All those who live on this earth have an instinctive fear of hunger. However, God promised that we would be fed.

"He who has an ear, let him hear what the Spirit says to the churches. To him who overcomes I will give to eat from the tree of life, which is in the midst of the Paradise of God."

Revelation 2:7

There are twelve brilliant gates for us to enter the wonderful kingdom of Heaven. God created these gates with unimaginable beauty.

"The twelve gates were twelve pearls: each individual gate was of one pearl. And the street of the city was pure gold, like transparent glass."

Revelation 21:21

The streets of gold, which extend from the gates, will be so pure that they are transparent. There will be perfect weather, but there will be no night and no sun. Do not worry about this because there will be God's beautiful, full, and natural light.

"The city had no need of the sun or of the moon to shine in it, for the glory of God illuminated it. The Lamb is its light. And the nations of those who are saved shall walk in its light, and the kings of the earth bring their glory and honor into it. Its gates shall not be shut at all by day (There shall be no night there)."

Revelation 21:23-25

God created the walls of Jerusalem with brilliant stones. The glory of God will cover the holy Jerusalem as it descends with brilliance, like an illustrious, magnificent stone, a stone that will shine like the pureness of crystal. However, its brilliance will outshine any precious gem we have ever seen on earth.

"The foundations of the wall of the city were adorned with all kinds of precious stones: the first foundation was jasper, the second sapphire, the third chalcedony, the fourth emerald, the fifth sardonic, the sixth sardius, the seventh crystallite, the eighth beryl, the ninth topaz, the tenth chrysoprase, the eleventh jacinth, and the twelfth amethyst."

Revelation 21:19-20

It is paradise, not only pleasing to the eye, where we will be with and see our beautiful God. Not just us, as we will reunite with our loved ones that have passed away.

There will be no judgment for those lucky enough to be there. God knows all our sins, but He has promised that He will forget them all and wipe all the tears from our eyes.

213

"They are before the throne of God and serve Him day and night in His temple. And He who sits on the throne will dwell among them. They shall neither hunger anymore nor thirst anymore; the sun shall not strike them, nor any heat; for the Lamb who is in the midst of the throne will shepherd them and lead them to living fountains of waters. And God will wipe away every tear from their eyes."

Revelation 7:15

Here is a plus for all you animal lovers out there. Many teachers of the Gospel also believe the animals we have loved and lost will go to heaven. Some theologians disagree and believe they cannot go because they have no "soul." Why not? Our dogs and cats have a soul – some are good, and some are bad. Once in, you can reunite with your beloved pets and favorite animals once again.

"If we have souls, our animals have souls."

Bekoff.

214

CONCLUSION

Life is tough.

None of us will ever sneak through it with ease. We all go through tough times. It is simply different things at various times. We all face schemes from evil people. Many attempt to steal our passwords or confidential information. Others sabotage us and set us up to look bad. Other, faceless people relish installing viruses on our computers. People like this do all they can to bring us challenging times.

Then there are other problems, like unexpected storm damage, diseases, hospitalizations, lost jobs, death of loved ones, financial difficulties, accidents, and on and on. We can conquer challenging times if we get our self-control back, using the methods in my first book, "Unleash Godly Power," and from this book. When living in demanding times, we must remain in complete control. We must collect ourselves and maintain mastery over ourselves and our emotions. We cannot take steps to work our way through it if we are full of anxiety and suffering from panic attacks. Only then can we define the problem(s) we are in and begin listing some alternative solutions. This may include seeking help from others.

The saying: "It never rains unless it pours," first appeared in the eighteenth century. There have always been tough times, but we can learn to prevent them and how best to deal with them. Going through challenging times is very painful for all of us. The worst thing we can do is to let a feeling of hopelessness take over and spend all day wallowing in our misery.

I have listed many serious problems in this book and suggested solutions to them. Remember: use this book as a reference book.

Put markers in sections you may need to refer to and use them when facing each challenge. At times, our problems will be so difficult that we will need the help of our church or counseling. Most problems do have solutions if we can calm down and work on them.

Be sure to keep your faith and ask God to help you get through this terrible period. Did you know that God is praying for us? If not, read the bible and do some research on this. We cannot do this on our own.

"Then they cried out to the LORD in their trouble, and he delivered them from their distress. He led them forth by the right way."

Psalm 107:28

He brings us safety, strength, encouragement, and hope. He becomes our shelter, refuge, and our strength. He will surround us with a shield of Armor to protect us from the Devil and his forces.

"Be strong and very courageous…be of good courage; do not be afraid, nor be dismayed for the Lord your God is with you wherever you go."

Joshua 1-9

Trials and tribulations will affect us all at one time or another. As I have said, this is not heaven. The only good side of these trials is that these demanding times make us stronger and better people. If we approach solutions with positive actions, our experience will mold us into the character that God intended us to have.

216

"Consider it pure joy, my brothers and sisters, whenever you face trials of many kinds."

James 1:2

"...the Spirit himself intercedes for us....Jesus is also interceding for us."

Romans 8:26-34

When we are in a good period without a huge crisis, we need to help others who are going through troubled times. There are many ways that we can help, depending upon our availability. Send a card. Text a joke. Give them a phone call. Buy them something. Bring them some food, or take them out to lunch. The amount of money you spend, or the amount of time, does not count. What is important is the thought that will help, even if you just sit with them and let them talk.

When each of us suffers from challenging times, we all feel hopeless, depressed, and helpless – but we can lift ourselves up and work our way out of the storms. We must keep our faith and remember that the sun and blue skies will return after the rain. Time heals all wounds; life is wonderful and full of joy and love if we live it as we should. The best things in life are free – so let us enjoy them.

Good luck.

Everything is going to be fine.

Godspeed.

SUGGESTED READING

"Unleash Godly Power" by Matt Jordan

"The Expectation Effect," by David Robson

"Holy Bible" (NIV preferred.)

"Spirit, Soul and Body" by Andrew Wommack

"The Power of Your Subconscious Mind," Joseph Murphy

"I Will," Ben Sweetland

" The True Nature of God," Andrew Wommack

"The Success Principles," Jack Canfield

"Don't Sweat the Small Stuff," Richard Carlson, PhD

"Tough Times Never Last, Tough People Do," Robert H. Schuller

"The Power of Positive Thinking," Dr. Norman Vincent Peale

"Battlefield of the Mind," Joyce Meyer

BOOK ORDER FORM

I would like to order _____ # of copies @ $9.95 each.

I add $3.00 shipping for each book, for a total of $ _____

Mail Check and Order to: Matt Jordan,

5 Flower Hill Road,

Poughkeepsie, N. Y. 12603

Your mailing address:

Name _____

Street _____

City _____ State _____ Zip _____

Phone Number _____ Cell _____

Email Address _____

Please contact me to discuss pricing for: (Check your choices)

Group lecture ____ Class or Seminar ____

Motivational Speech ___ Prvate counseling ____

By Phone ___ Email ___ Personal Meeting ___ Date _____

For any other questions or difficulty ordering, Please Email:

mjordan423@gmail.com

219